T0340211

Cultures of Violence

Investigating art practitioners' responses to violence, this book considers how artists have used art practices to rethink concepts of violence and non-violence. It explores the strategies that artists have deployed to expose physical and symbolic violence through representational, performative and interventional means.

It examines how intellectual and material contexts have affected art interventions and how visual arts can open up critical spaces to explore violence without reinforcement or recuperation. Its premises are that art is not only able to contest prevailing norms about violence but that contemporary artists are consciously engaging with publics through their practice in order to do so. Contributors respond to three questions: how can political violence be understood or interpreted through art? How are publics understood or identified? How are art interventions designed to shift, challenge or respond to public perceptions of political violence and how are they constrained by them? They discuss violence in the everyday and at state level: the Watts' Rebellion and Occupy, repression in Russia, domination in Hong Kong, the violence of migration and the unfolding art activist logic of the *sigma portfolio*.

Asking how public debates can be shaped through the visual and performing arts and setting taboos about violence to one side, the volume provides an innovative approach to a perennial issue of interest to scholars of international politics, art and cultural studies.

Ruth Kinna works at Loughborough University in the School of Social Sciences and Humanities as a political theorist and historian of ideas.

Gillian Whiteley is Senior Lecturer in Art History and Visual Culture at Loughborough University and co-organiser of RadicalAesthetics-RadicalArt.

Interventions
Edited by Jenny Edkins
Aberystwyth University

Nick Vaughan-Williams
University of Warwick

The Series provides a forum for innovative and interdisciplinary work that engages with alternative critical, post-structural, feminist, postcolonial, psychoanalytic and cultural approaches to international relations and global politics. In our first 5 years we have published 60 volumes.

We aim to advance understanding of the key areas in which scholars working within broad critical post-structural traditions have chosen to make their interventions, and to present innovative analyses of important topics. Titles in the series engage with critical thinkers in philosophy, sociology, politics and other disciplines and provide situated historical, empirical and textual studies in international politics.

We are very happy to discuss your ideas at any stage of the project: just contact us for advice or proposal guidelines. Proposals should be submitted directly to the Series Editors:

- Jenny Edkins (jennyedkins@hotmail.com) and
- Nick Vaughan-Williams (N.Vaughan-Williams@Warwick.ac.uk).

'As Michel Foucault has famously stated, "knowledge is not made for understanding; it is made for cutting". In this spirit The Edkins–Vaughan-Williams Interventions series solicits cutting edge, critical works that challenge mainstream understandings in international relations. It is the best place to contribute post disciplinary works that think rather than merely recognize and affirm the world recycled in IR's traditional geopolitical imaginary.'

Michael J. Shapiro, University of Hawai'i at Manoa, USA

Nation-branding in Practice
The Politics of Promoting Sports, Cities and Universities in Kazakhstan and Qatar
Kristin Anabel Eggeling

Cultures of Violence
Visual Arts and Political Violence
Edited by Ruth Kinna and Gillian Whiteley

For more information about this series, please visit: www.routledge.com/series/INT

Cultures of Violence
Visual Arts and Political Violence

**Edited by Ruth Kinna
and Gillian Whiteley**

Routledge
Taylor & Francis Group

LONDON AND NEW YORK

First published 2020
by Routledge
2 Park Square, Milton Park, Abingdon, Oxon OX14 4RN

and by Routledge
52 Vanderbilt Avenue, New York, NY 10017

Routledge is an imprint of the Taylor & Francis Group, an informa business

British Library Cataloguing-in-Publication Data
A catalogue record for this book is available from the British Library

Library of Congress Cataloging-in-Publication Data
Names: Kinna, Ruth, editor. | Whiteley, Gillian, editor.
Title: Cultures of violence : visual arts and political violence / edited by
    Ruth Kinna and Gillian Whiteley.
Other titles: Cultures of violence (Routledge (Firm))
Description: Abingdon, Oxon ; New York, NY : Routledge, 2020. | Series:
    Interventions | Includes bibliographical references and index.
Identifiers: LCCN 2020003109 (print) | LCCN 2020003110 (ebook) |
    ISBN 9781138624917 (hardback) | ISBN 9780429460357 (ebook)
Subjects: LCSH: Art—Political aspects. | Art and social action. | Political
    violence.
Classification: LCC N72.P6 C85 2020 (print) | LCC N72.P6 (ebook) |
    DDC 701/.03—dc23
LC record available at https://lccn.loc.gov/2020003109
LC ebook record available at https://lccn.loc.gov/2020003110

ISBN: 978-1-138-62491-7 (hbk)
ISBN: 978-0-367-49753-8 (pbk)
ISBN: 978-0-429-46035-7 (ebk)

Typeset in Times New Roman
by Apex CoVantage, LLC

Contents

Contributors

The editors

Ruth Kinna works at Loughborough University in the School of Social Sciences and Humanities as a political theorist and historian of ideas. Her research focuses on anarchism and radical politics. Her most recent book is *The Government of No One* (Pelican, 2019). Her collaboration with Gillian Whiteley started in Gillian's Politicised Practice Research Group. With Gillian and Fred Dalmasso she helped launch Critical Citizenship and Art Activism (www.pparg.net) and the ongoing project Re-imagining Citizenship, which exhibited at the Venice Biennale, 2019.

Gillian Whiteley is Senior Lecturer in Art History and Visual Culture at Loughborough University and co-organiser of RadicalAesthetics-RadicalArt. Recent publications include 'From Being One to Being-in-Common: Political Performativity, Proxemics, and the Joys of Provisional Unity' in *Performance Matters* (Winter 2018). Current projects include the collaborative initiative Re-imagining Citizenship/Living Archive at www.re-imagining.org and *Art, Politics and the Pamphleteer* (forthcoming Bloomsbury). For more info see www.bricolagekitchen.com

The contributors

Amy Corcoran is a visual artist and researcher whose doctoral research investigated the use of public art interventions to support migrant justice struggles within the recent EU context. Amy's published writing primarily centres on the policing of protest and her experiences and reflections on the unfolding situation in Calais, France. The majority of Amy's own art practice is politically and environmentally motivated, though its medium is varied and includes performance, installation and illustration.

Jessica Holtaway's research centres on politically-engaged artworks and performances. She is interested in the relationship between creativity and crisis. She recently completed a PhD in the Department of Visual Cultures at Goldsmiths with a thesis that explored micropolitical art interventions through reading the philosophy of Jean-Luc Nancy. Jessica is a co-editor of the book *artWORK: Art, Labour and Activism* (published by Rowman and Littlefield International in 2017). She is a currently Lecturer in the School of Art, Design and Fashion at Solent University.

Jaakko Karhunen is a scholar, artist and organiser. Currently at Loughborough University, he is defending his PhD thesis on Félix Guattari's late philosophy of subjectivity in January 2020. For the past two years he has been leading an artistic research project, *Reading the Enemies*, funded by the Kone Foundation. The project consists of workshops where researchers, artists and activists have been giving readings about their own theoretical and political adversaries. He is also editing two academic journal issues on the topic of the project. He has presented his work in international conferences, journals and exhibitions and has taken part in various artist-in-residency programs. He holds an MFA degree from the Finnish Academy of Fine Arts (2009).

Martin Lang is an artist and a writer. His research specialises in militancy in art activism. He has published research on militancy, the neo-avantgarde, revolution and the apocalypse in journals such as *Art & the Public Sphere*, *Krisis* and *Ekphrasis*. He also writes for *Trebuchet Magazine*. He is currently working on a book, entitled *Militant Aesthetics: Art Activism in the 21st Century* and an exhibition about truth and painting. He is Senior Lecturer in Fine Art at the University of Lincoln, where he co-leads the MA in fine art.

Marina Maximova is a historian of late-Soviet and post-Soviet art and culture. She is currently Lecturer in Art Business at Sotheby's Institute of Art. Previously she taught in Loughborough University School of Art. Marina's research focuses on Russian and Eastern European art and markets, collecting and exhibition histories. Her doctoral thesis explored experimental curatorial practices in late-Soviet Russia. Outside of academia Marina worked in a variety of cultural organisations in Moscow and in London, including Garage Museum of Contemporary Art, Tate Modern and Gazelli Art House.

Vlad Morariu is a researcher, curator and Lecturer in Visual Cultures at Middlesex University London. His doctoral thesis (2014, Loughborough University) explored the conditions and possibilities of art practices of institutional critique. In 2016 he was AHRC Cultural Engagement Fellow, with a project that revisited Scottish psychiatrist R.D. Laing's reading of phenomenology and its importance within the therapeutic communities that Laing co-established in London in the 1960s. Vlad's current research focuses on transformative semiotic practices in contemporary art. Together with Raluca Voinea and Judit Angel he co-initiated *Collection Collective*, an international network of artists, curators and cultural organisers, who in 2017 founded a collection of contemporary art, collectively owned and managed by its members.

Acknowledgments

We would like to thank our contributors for their commitment and the Independent Social Research Foundation for funding the two-day workshop on Art, Activism and Political Violence, which brought us all together. We would particularly like to thank Stuart Wilson at the ISRF for all his help and support throughout the project. Thanks, too, to James Ellison, Woldegorgis Ghebrehiwot, Klaudia Kaleta, Adam Kossoff, Irina Kunetsova, Theo Price and Stevphen Shukaitis, who also participated in the workshop and helped us think about the issues discussed in this book and to Bernadette Buckley for her encouragement and enthusiasm. We are enormously grateful to our series editors, Jenny Edkins and Nick Vaughan-Williams, for being so patient with us and to Robert Sorsby at Routledge for his flexibility and advice.

Introduction

'Art, culture and violence'

Ruth Kinna and Gillian Whiteley

Aims and premises

This short collection explores art practitioners' responses to violence. It considers how artists have used art practices to rethink the nature of violence and non-violence, and it examines how intellectual and material contexts have affected and shaped art interventions. Its premises are that art is not only able to contest prevailing norms about violence but that contemporary artists are consciously engaging with publics through their practice in order to do so. By foregrounding the communicative, public interventions artists make in highly ideologically charged situations and to sometimes abstruse philosophical discussions, our aim is to prompt reflection about political violence, namely the use of violence to advance political causes or to express political dissent.

The essays were originally presented at a two-day workshop entitled Art, Activism and Political Violence.[1] Contributors were asked to address three questions: how can political violence be understood or interpreted through art? How are publics understood or identified? How are art interventions designed to shift, challenge or respond to public perceptions of political violence and/or are constrained by them? In different ways, each presentation tackled the moralisation of violence and the power-plays involved in the legitimisation and demonisation of actions and processes. Yet rather than settle on definitions of any of our key terms, our contributors have advanced a range of conceptions. Politics is variously understood as an engagement in or for the creation of alternative public spheres and as a social relationship structured by power inequalities. Likewise, violence is described as a system of oppression, a disciplining power and/or an atmosphere described by emergency, the stifling of creativity, habitual performance, as well as subjection to physical harm. The focus of the discussion is broadly contemporary: our contributors consider interventions that extend back to the 1960s and current activity. They explore the work of artists who operate in very different geographical areas and historical-political contexts: case studies discuss artists who enjoy more or less freedom of expression, confront varying degrees of social conflict and risk different levels of harm to themselves and the publics they work with.

The close relationship of art and politics elicits a plurality of views about the incidence of violence, its harms and effects and appropriate strategies for its resistance. Describing cultural resistance as a response to political violence, Martin Lang presents a fifty year history of transatlantic activism, from the 1965 Watts Rebellion in Los Angeles to the global Occupy movement of 2011 to reflect on division and unity in activist struggles. Marina Maximova similarly treats the emergence of Moscow Actionism in the 1990s as a response to violence, in this case prompted by the collapse of the Soviet regime and transformation of social life under the new capitalist, marketised order. Yet approaching strategy from the perspective of public space, she considers how far the movement re-imagined space in the streets and the press in post-Soviet Russia.

The collection also presents us with alternative approaches to 'art activism'. Vlad Morariu and Jaakko Karhunen discuss *sigma* – a network of cultural practitioners active in the 1960s – and the *sigma portfolio*, its most tangible achievement, to develop an exemplar of art activism. Examining a plethora of interventions designed to reveal and contest the state violence implicit in bordering and migration, Amy Corcoran outlines a set of possible relationships between artists and activism to advance a flexible model of art as an instrument of social change. Jessica Holtaway's discussion of *Hong Kong Intervention*, an artwork that invited migrant domestic workers to place a toy grenade in their employers' homes, pursues a related idea of art as a transformative practice. Yet she demonstrates how the potential of art depends on the antagonistic engagements that it generates. The cultural spaces that art inhabits are thus also central to its political affect.

Artists have long deployed a range of strategies to expose both physical and symbolic violence through representational, performative and interventional means. In the last 100 years, industrial, bureaucratised terror, war and its social effects have informed much of this work. For centuries though, traditional artforms were funded or appropriated by the state to support war, colonial expansion and justify various forms of political, structural and systemic violence. As W.J.T. Mitchell has indicated, a good deal of the world's public art – memorials, monuments, triumphal arches, obelisks, columns and statues – has a direct reference to violence in the form of war or conquest and has served as a kind of 'monumentalizing of violence' (Mitchell, 1990). Of course, there have been notable exceptions: Maya Lin's *Vietnam Veterans War Memorial* (1982) subverted the tradition of the phallic column and challenged the glorification of war through its black granite minimalist forms. The 'counter-monuments' against fascism, war and violence, 'designed not to console but to provoke', produced by Hans Haacke and Jochen Gerz in the 1980s and 1990s, are other important examples (Stevens et al., 2012: 952).

The representation of scenes or acts of violence raises complex aesthetic and ethical issues for both artist and spectator. Religious art of earlier centuries was replete with depictions of excruciating scenes of physical violence and cruelty; witness Matthias Grünewald's Isenheim Altarpiece or the gruesome images in Hieronymous Bosch's work, a forewarning of the tortures awaiting the morally 'fallen' in hell. The twentieth century presented its own earthly hells with artists searching for new approaches to re-present the horrors, from Picasso's deployment of earlier Cubist abstract forms to convey mass suffering in his monumental *Guernica* (1937) to Peter de Francia's lesser-known 'social realist' painting *The Bombing of Sakiet* (1959), depicting the mass killing of civilians by French colonial forces in Algeria (Hyman, 2001). Although employing a very different aesthetic, these were socially engaged 'committed' artists, keen to expose state and structural violence to a wider public through artistic forms of representation.

The problems of re-presenting violence through imagery are multifarious. Theodor Adorno's oft-quoted comment that 'to write poetry after Auschwitz is barbaric' (Adorno, 1967: 34) continues to resonate with the dilemma facing artists and writers who want to deal with barely conceivable horror through cultural forms. How can the un-showable be shown through artforms with which we generally associate aesthetic contemplation? In his study of violence, Slavoj Žižek argues that there is something inherently mystifying in a direct confrontation with it and warns that the overpowering horror of violent acts and empathy with the victims inexorably function as '*a lure* which prevents us thinking' (Žižek, 2009: 3). In an age in which photographic images have proliferated profusely, well beyond the mechanical means that Walter Benjamin highlighted as problematic in the 1930s (Benjamin [1935] in Arndt, 1969), the constant reproduction and reiteration of brutalising imagery through various media may well be the 'lure' that prevents us thinking by dulling its effect on the viewer. Andy Warhol's reiterations of appropriated car crash scenes in his 'death and disaster' series of the 1960s, viewed alongside J.G. Ballard's iconic experimental novel *The Atrocity Exhibition* (1969), convey a fascination with mid-century psychic violence and an urge to shock audiences out of their dumb complacency. Earnestly, without irony, the explicit photographic works of Santiago Sierra and Alfredo Jaar (Batchen et al., 2012) have gone further in their representation. Whilst aiming to confront and comment on 'atrocity' resulting from political violence, the excess of affect their images create ends up being counter-productive. It reproduces another layer of violence, not only objectifying and victimising those who suffer but, in the process, inuring and making complicit those who are doing the looking.

One solution, found in the 1960s and 70s, was to reject representational approaches altogether along with traditional artforms and, instead of producing an art object, create environments, durational events and performances. In particular, the artist's own body operated as a site of the political in performative interventions that have commonly been interpreted as responses to political violence, state-sponsored brutality and warfare. Performances were often disturbing ordeals for artist and viewer. In 1966, in the basement of Better Books on Charing Cross Road, Jeff Nuttall and others spent months building the *sTigma* environment, a labyrinthine assemblage of photographic material, found objects, violent and sexual imagery and dripping, decaying matter, including human flesh: the idea was to force visitors to squeeze through the material, directly experiencing the horrors of war through a disturbing and affective physical encounter (Whiteley, 2011). In the States, Chris Burden, inspired by the nightly TV news footage of young men getting killed in Vietnam, famously had himself shot (1971); in *Transfixed* (1974) he was nailed to the top on the roof of a Volkswagen Beetle. In Brazil in 1969 over the course of six months, Artur Barrio placed hundreds of bloody bundles of rotting flesh in public locations for people to discover unwittingly, with a view to provoking outrage at the military regime's brutal elimination of political activists (Calirman, 2012). Responding directly to allegations in the *Irish Times* of torture methods used by the British Army to extract confessions from Republican prisoners in Northern Ireland, in *And for today . . . nothing* (1972) the British artist Stuart Brisley immersed his body in a bath full of cold water with rotting offal and maggots hatching in it for ten days, drifting between drowning and sinking (Williams, 2015). This visceral act of endurance rivalled the actions of Hermann Nitsch and the Viennese Actionists and their legendary performances such as *Art and Revolution* (1968) or Otto Muehl's *Manopsychotic Ballet* (1970), a transgressive work only recently reinserted into art's histories (Ursprung, 2019). Directly referencing the kinds of bodily traumas perpetrated under National Socialism, these radical performances frequently incorporated acts of extreme physical and mental exhaustion, sexual violence, masochism, mutilation, defecation and the devouring of animals (Weiner, 2015).

Through the 1980s and 1990s, the body continued to offer a site for transgressive performance with artists such as Marina Abramovic and Andre Stitt carrying out extreme acts of self-inflicted pain and mutilation that sometimes left audiences traumatised (Stitt, 2001). Clearly, the use and abuse of the artist's classed, gendered, racialised body in performative actions continues to raise new ethical and political questions, as the Chinese dissident artist Ai Weiwei found to his disadvantage when he published a photograph in which he posed as a drowned refugee child on the seashore (ahead of his documentary film in 2017). Presented as a well-meaning act of empathy and identification, it was widely condemned by critics as self-indulgent, highlighting only too well some of the pitfalls and complexities surrounding these kinds of practices (Jones, 2016).

More recently, new interrogations of violence have been stimulated by repeated waves of protest and struggles against unjust and oppressive systems. The routine experience of austerity, migration and repression provide an important backdrop. Our contention is that the sustained deployment of exclusionary discourses by politicians designed to delineate 'the people' from its enemies – outsiders who threaten romanticised social norms – make the exploration of these art practices not only timely but urgent. In a period when, as one commentator put it, the 'blood-stained' remains of various victims of violence are turned into 'deeply ugly' resources for all manner of 'shallow political causes' (O'Neill, 2016), art can help us examine the mechanics of political violence and expose the ways that threats of harm are used to instil fear and stifle creative thinking. We develop this line of argument later. We do this first by explaining our understanding of politicised practice. This helps us locate the chapters in the collection and consider how intellectual borrowing can broaden our theoretical perspectives, enabling us to reimagine our social relationships and the character of the violence they structure. Second, we unpack the conjunction of 'culture' and 'violence' to advance an idea of violence as a permanent condition, not an interruption of 'normal' social processes. The final section considers how contemporary art practices' interrogations of violence have been stimulated by the global resurgence of multiple forms of 'creative dissent' (McQuiston, 2015) and 'cultural resistance' (Duncombe, 2002).

Interdisciplinarity and 'politicised practice'

Interdisciplinarity is 'an easy world and a challenging concept' (Alessiato, 2014: 1). In a general sense, it assumes the existence of discrete branches of knowledge as a starting point and 'refers to an activity that exists among existing disciplines or in a reciprocal relationship between them' (Alvargonzález, 2011: 388). However, rather than accept the boundedness of each scholarly discipline as a starting-point (Apter, 2010: 183), we have assumed their interrelationship. In other words, we understand the broad fields of art and politics as 'quasi-stable, partially integrated, semi-autonomous' 'thought domains' that have core and peripheral elements as well as highly specialised sub-fields (Aram, 2004: 380). This approach allows us to describe what we mean by politicised practice or socially engaged art and outline the relationship between politicised practice and the political theory.

Following Aram, we treat politicised practice as a field of 'instrumental interdisciplinarity'. That is, we acknowledge that contributors to this volume already 'utilize or borrow the ideas or methods' from cognate fields 'to enhance problem solving within their home disciplines' (Aram, 2004: 382). The character of politicised practice reflects a commitment to social change typical of other interdisciplinary studies, for example women's studies, peace studies, environmental studies and African American studies.

The relationship between politicised practice and political theory emerges from an effort to exploit and develop a tight 'linking of disciplines'. Our invitation to ask questions about the constitution of violence and the possibility of affecting or changing public debates acknowledges the 'independence of each discipline' (Alvargonzález, 2011: 388) but also the shared spaces that art practitioners and political theorists inhabit. We appreciate that scholars schooled in separate disciplines approach the conceptualisation and analysis of violence differently, draw on diverse canons and bodies of thought or practice and promote 'different epistemologies and methods' (Schoenberger, 2001: 367). Yet maintaining the distance in this relationship also means treating politicised practice and political theory as shared cultures. Politicised practice and political theory are linked by 'common, attitudes, common standards and patterns of behavior, common approaches and assumptions' (Snow quoted in Schoenberger, 2001: 367). There are also commonalities in ways of 'thinking about the material and social world', 'in the identification of "objects" of study' and in the 'abstractions' used to analyse them (Schoenberger, 2001: 371). Art practitioners and political theorists share similar critical perspectives on the issue of violence. All the chapters in the collection make this point very clearly. Yet our authors are not constrained by political theory conventions precisely because the exploration and application of ideas takes priority over conceptual or textual analysis and interpretation. This form of interdisciplinarity is productive because it allows art practitioners to hold a mirror to political theory and generate insights that political theorists can treat as 'reliable knowledge' (Schoenberger, 2001: 368).

Edward Hyams' application of consequentialism to imaginatively reverse the logic of arguments about the justness of violence is an example. In *Killing no Murder* (1970) Hyams blended mythology and Freudian psychology with sociology and politics to present a public good defence of political assassination. Accepting the power asymmetries between leaders and the led, he argued for the revival of scapegoating and endorsed the right of tyrannicide to preserve social well-being. By his estimation of harm, these were far better alternatives than the mass slaughter engendered by war. As a veteran of the Second World War and self-confessed killer, he explained:

Political and military leaders, no longer reared in a tradition of leader self-sacrifice, no longer accepting the idea and feeling that the chieftain must fight in front of his people, and not behind them, would naturally be far more anxious to keep the peace if their lives were first to be endangered by war, and their survival unlikely. And to put it in terms more honourable to these mighty men, the assassination, one after another of leaders as they rose courageously to take the places of the already assassinated, could not but bring war to an end much sooner if it be true, as such leaders themselves believe, that the number of men capable of effective leadership is very limited.

(Hyams, 1970: 39)

Hyams was forbidden by his publishers from detailing his own list of world leaders deserving of assassination. But there was no need to reveal it, for the point was to imagine its construction, not to operationalise it. *Killing no Murder* was an artistic exercise, not a manifesto. Hyams borrowed a familiar framing of violence, namely the 'ticking timebomb scenario', which invites students of politics to consider the utility of torturing captives believed to have information about lethal devices for the sake of public safety. The thought experiment is routinely used to justify the use of torture, despite its obvious flaws. Hyams used it to say the unsayable, produce dissensus – possibly outrage – and re-imagine existing power relations. Recognising the durability if not inevitability of hierarchy and power inequality, he set prejudices about rightful authority to one side and invited his readers to rethink the rightness of killing.

Culture and violence

Placing two complex, disputed concepts alongside each other seems ill-advised and perhaps confusing. Ill-advised because of the vastness of the literature exploring the meanings of 'culture' and 'violence' and confusing because everyday usages of 'culture' encourage us to frame 'violence' as a special event or moment, an aberration of our usual practices and a threat to our collective achievements. Violence carries many associations including, for example, the practices of Mafia gangs (Schneider and Schneider, 1994; Parker, 2008), ritualised gender violence in non-European communities (Adelman, Haldane and Wies, 2012) and state failure (Kaplan, 1994, 2018). All of these are troubling and controversial, yet each illustrates how the juxtaposition of violence and culture typically jars. It is surely unfitting to conjoin these terms when describing 'normal', 'civilised' social arrangements?

The conception of violence as a disruptive event runs through much of the literature on the ethics of violence. As Frazer and Hutching note (2019:

1–16), it is not possible to pass judgments about legitimacy without determining what constitutes violence in the first place. And political philosophers are wont to probe this question by assuming or developing contrasting notions of order or peace. The contrast, grounded in law, is by no means straightforward. As Christoph Menke observes, 'the relation between law and violence' is contradictory: 'law is both the opposite of violence' and 'is itself violence' (Menke, 2018: 3). By subjecting citizens equally to the fear of judgment, it fixes procedures, norms, rules and principles for social interaction (ibid.: 20–1). Thus 'politics' is sometimes constructed as a sphere of freedom obliterated by violence or a regulated order facilitating escape from an imagined place of violent disorder through the creation of government. Likewise, following Kant, the international sphere is commonly theorised as a realm of potential perpetual peace, achievable by the extension of liberal constitutionalism and cosmopolitan law (Danilovic and Clare, 2007).

Sociological analysis complicates this view, typically linking the brutality and aggression involved in the actual establishment of political authority with the normalisation of dominating practices. Achille Mbembe's critique of colonialism blurs the stark contrast between social peace and a-social violence by distinguishing 'founding violence' or the 'right of conquest' and 'the prerogatives flowing' from it from 'legitimation' and 'cultural violence'. The latter processes give meaning to colonial orders and so perpetuate them by means other than 'war' (Mbembe, 2001: 25). Žižek's conceptual model works similarly. Here, violence refers both to the subjective actions of a 'clearly identifiable agent' and to less visible and 'symbolic' and 'systemic' processes, namely, the 'violence embodied in language' and the 'catastrophic consequences of the smooth functioning of our economic and political systems' (Žižek, 2009: 1). In both cases, violence is construed as part of our social experience, more or less visible and more or less accepted but felt differently by particular groups and individuals. For Black women, Audre Lorde explained,

> violence weaves through the daily tissue of our living – in the supermarket, in the classroom, in the elevator, in the clinic and the schoolyard, from the plumber, the baker, the saleswoman, the bus driver, the bank teller, the waitress who does not serve us.
>
> (Lorde, 2007: 119)

Recognising the permanence of violence helps focus attention on the conditions and mechanisms likely to intensify or diminish its repressive character. In the past, scholars of development have inversely linked structural violence, the violence 'legitimized by the prevailing juricidal order and sociopolitical and economic institutions', to levels of equality and disparities of power, wealth and income. High differentials point to strong 'systems of coercion, suppression and intensive internal security' and 'rigid, inflexible political structures' that leave 'little room' for conflict resolution (Gunatelleke, Tiruchelvan and Coomaraswamy, 1983: 132–3). Following slightly different lines of investigation, anthropologists have compared social orders by describing the mechanisms used by power-holders to control and manage violence, for example, rumour, sorcery and spectacle (Strathern and Stewart, 2006: 1–39). By examining how 'performers, victims and witnesses' respond to particular actions, they show that questions of meaning and legitimacy are fluid and contestable (ibid.: 5). From this perspective, the designation of an act as 'violent' is part of a general contestation of power. In this, performers, victims and witnesses will often perceive violence differently. The subjectivity of evaluation was noted by the nineteenth-century ethnographer Elie Reclus. In a discussion of the impact of westward expansion on the Native Americans, he observed that Apache 'cruelty' proved to be the more powerful point of reference for 'violence' than the Washington land policy that fenced off First Nation hunting grounds, reducing the population by a quarter in a sixty-year period (Reclus, n.d.: 141). Fleshing out the analysis, Pamela Stewart and Andrew Strathern explain:

> The issue of violence turns on the question of whose perception of order is at stake. Violence pinpoints the differences between people's perceptions of what is proper and appropriate in different contexts of conflict. This explains why it is praised by some and condemned by others. The perception for what is violence may also be subjective. Alternatively people may agree on what constitutes violence but disagree on whether it is appropriate or justified.
>
> (Stewart and Strathern, 2002: 3)

Struggles to decode violence operate on the level of imagination as well as by 'everyday empirical observations' (Strathern and Stewart, 2006: 7). They are fundamentally about meaning and rationality, where rationality and meaningfulness centre on legal norms, albeit detached from issues of evaluation. People often disagree about the rightness of legal violence but do not usually question its meaningfulness or rationality. Finding the meaningfulness or rationality in actions that fall outside the law is usually much harder. The designation of terrorism is a marker of unintelligibility, inversely related to the perceived rationality of official response. But there are other familiar markers. Stewart and Strathern find the limits to rationality in anarchism: self-identifying anarchists fall outside the legal order and their violence is by implication meaningless (Stewart and Strathern,

2002: 3). However, having drawn attention to the cultural contexts in which violence is constructed, their anthropologically-inflected approach to violence suggests that meanings can always be decoded. Simultaneously acknowledging and challenging the conventional framing of violence as a disruptive event, Anton Blok argues: 'Rather than defining violence *a priori* as senseless and irrational we should consider it as a changing form of interaction and communication, as a historically developed cultural form of *meaningful* action' (Blok, 2001: 104).

Social movement scholars have adopted Blok's approach to decipher the meanings of protest actions and highlight the readiness of performers to risk significant harm as part of their actions. Analysing the black bloc at the 2001 anti-G8 protest in Genoa, Jeffrey Juris shows how systematic mainstream media dismissals of activists as hooligans reinforced the meaninglessness of the protesters' actions and paved the way for extraordinary police aggression (Juris, 2005). Yet black bloc activists used violence symbolically and instrumentally to build solidarities across marginalised and dominated groups, imagine alternative social arrangements and draw mainstream media attention to anticapitalist critique:

> young militants in Genoa generated potent oppositional identities and communicated a radical antisystemic critique by enacting prototypical scenes of youth rebellion against the symbols of global capitalism and the state. Indeed, performative violence is neither random nor senseless, but rather responds to a specific economy of signification. The resulting mass media images helped bring a great deal of public visibility to anti-corporate globalization movements, and even to many of their political demands.
>
> (ibid.: 427)

For critics, the intelligibility of violence cannot serve as a justification. Arguing that violence is anyway usually counterproductive, Frazer and Hutchings argue that it can never make things right and that the conditions that make political violence can never by justified (2019: 121). Yet if this is the case, the relationship between culture and violence helps us understand the contexts in which violence operates, the forms it takes and the judgments it elicits. It also teaches us to explore the passions that motivate it. Lorde's distinction of hate from anger is especially pertinent. 'Hatred is the fury of those who do not share our goals, and its object is death and destruction. Anger is a grief of distortions between peers, and its object is change' (2007 [1984]: 129). Hatred described racism; anger was its appropriate reaction, 'as is fury when the actions arising from those attitudes do not change' (ibid.). Anger alone, Lorde admitted, can 'only demolish the past' it 'cannot create the future'. Yet unlike hatred, which is destructive and 'necessarily harmful', anger can only 'be excessive or misplaced' (152). Lorde was not attempting to justify violence. But her recognition of these passions left the conversation about violence open and indeed encouraged its interrogation.

> The angers between women will not kill us if we can articulate them with precision, if we listen to the content of what is said with at least as much intensity as we defend ourselves against the manner of saying. When we turn from anger we turn from insight, saying we will accept only the designs already known, deadly and safely familiar. I have tried to learn my anger's usefulness to me, as well as its limitations.
>
> (131)

Situating art practice now

While more traditional forms of artistic representation have found less favour in contemporary practices, historical motifs that designate physical violence and political violation are frequently reiterated and recycled. In 1948, looking back to the tyranny of the Inquisition through the lens of the Spanish Civil War, Francis Klingender brought a Marxist reading to Goya's images of torture, physical constraint, sensory deprivation and imprisonment (Klingender, 1968). These have continued to inform imagery to this day, not just via the work of artists such as Jake and Dinos Chapman but through their echo in the disturbing photographs of hooded and manacled prisoners at Abu Ghraib. Images that, in turn and with an ironic twist, have been replicated in graphic works such as *iRaq* (produced by Forkscrew Graphics). This now iconic downloadable poster appropriated the silhouette of a hooded prisoner being tortured, whilst subverting stylistic elements from Apple's iPod ad campaigns (McQuiston, 2015: 115). In May 2004, particular parallels were drawn with Goya's images after print media published photographs of tortured Iraqis at Abu Ghraib. In *The Abu Ghraib Effect*, Stephen Eisenman explores how such images of torture, power and domination pass down the generations and become embedded, not only in visual memory but also, he argues, in the physical body (Eisenman, 2007: 38–9).

In the twenty-first century, contemporary artists continue to work with performative practices and interventions that are provocative and confrontational, sometimes staging horrific acts that dupe audiences and publics into confusing fiction with reality. A prime case is the Iraqi artist Wafaa Bilal's project *Domestic Tension* (2007) (documented in his book *I Shoot an Iraqi*, 2008). His projects grapple with his experience of living through the brutalities of Saddam Hussein's regime and surviving the Gulf War attacks but, at the same time, critically interrogate the mediation of violence through digital technology and gaming cultures (Unger, 2015). Elsewhere, other artists raise awareness of political violence more powerfully, not through showing or telling but, more obliquely, through working with absences and invisibility, a strategy adopted by the Mexican artist Teresa Margolles, whose work *Sonidos de la muerte* (*Sounds of Death*) (2008) addresses cultures of death and violence in contemporary Mexico. Other art projects may take a more communal collaborative approach as in the various community art projects featured in *Artivism: the Atrocity Prevention Pavilion* at the Venice Biennale (2019). In contrast, over the last couple of decades, there has been a merging of direct action, street politics and practices formerly associated with art. McQuiston describes 'a crossing or blurring of boundaries between creative fields of practice, particularly when dealing with social and political messages of dissent' and classic formats such as posters, paintings, photographs, films and performances that are now just as likely to be in a gallery as on the side of a building (McQuiston, 2015: 9). Humour, as opposed to earnest fervour, constantly features in various forms of 'creative dissent' in the activities of groups like the Clown Army and PopMob or the playful strategies promoted by Sroja Popovic in his 'handbook' *Blueprint for Revolution: how to use rice pudding, lego men and other non-violent techniques to galvanise communities, overthrow dictators, or simply change the world* (Popovic, 2015).

Despite the pitfalls and complexities, a good deal of art has retained its capacity to affect, to critique and to imagine other possible worlds. More importantly for the kinds of politicised interventions and socially-engaged practices outlined in this book, art increasingly functions as a site for the generation of debate and facilitation of conversations about difficult and taboo topics in public contexts. Accepting that art functions in a reality 'deeply penetrated by capitalist relations and limitations' and that artistic and cultural modes of production are just as subject to 'capture' as any other modes (Kurant, Sowa and Szadkowski, 2014 : 250, 254), nevertheless, we maintain that thinking about art's cultural and social impact in relation to questions of violence and assessing its transformative potential in the real world remains of paramount concern.

The idea that violence is malleable to context and that it has the potential to construct and re-shape social relationships similarly helps us situate art as part of a culture of violence. Artists can reproduce established ways of thinking, reinforcing what is conventionally said and thought about violence. As Chantal Mouffe argues, even critical work is readily recuperated (Mouffe, 2007). Yet artists can equally disrupt or disturb exiting conventions by creating dissensus and constantly invent resources to resist co-optation

(Shapiro, 2013: xv; Minor Compositions, n.d.). Perhaps the interdisciplinary nature of art gives artists peculiar latitude to do this.

Note

1 Hosted at Loughborough University and funded by the Independent Social Research Foundation, Small Group Project April-August 2016 www.isrf.org/about/fellows-and-projects/fg2-1/.

Bibliography

Adelman, Madelaine, Hillary Haldane and Jennifer R. Wies. 'Mobilizing Culture as an Asset: A Transdisciplinary Effort to Rethink Gender Violence', *Violence Against Women* 18 (16) (2012), 691–700.

Adorno, Theodor. 'Culture, Criticism and Society', in *Prisms* (trans. and introduction S. & S. Weber) (London: Neville Spearman, 1967).

Alessiato, Elena. 'Does a Method for Interdisciplinarity Exist?', *Journal of Interdisciplinary History of Ideas* 3 (2014), 1–21.

Alvargonzález, David. 'Multidiciplinarity, Interdisciplinarity, Transdisciplinarity, and the Sciences', *International Studies in the Philosophy of Science*, 25 (4) (2011), 387–403.

Apter, David. 'An Approach to Interdisciplinarity', *International Social Science Journal*, 196 (2010), 183–93.

Aram, John. 'Concepts of Interdisciplinarity: Configurations of Knowledge and Action', *Human Relations*, 57 (4) (2004), 379–412.

Ballard, J.G. *The Atrocity Exhibition* [1969] (London: Fourth Estate, 2014).

Batchen, Geoffrey et al. (eds.). *Picturing Atrocity: Photography in Crisis* (London: Reaktion, 2012).

Benjamin, Walter. 'The Work of Art in the Age of Mechanical Reproduction' [orig. published in German, 1935], in Arendt, Hannah (ed.), *Illuminations* (trans. Harry Zohn) (New York: Schocken Books, 1969).

Blok, Anton. *Honour and Violence* (Oxford and Cambridge: Polity Press, 2001).

Calirman, Claudia. *Brazilian Art Under Dictatorship: Antonio Manuel, Artur Barrio, and Cildo Meireles* (Durham: Duke University Press, 2012).

Danilovic, Vesna and Joe Clare. 'The Kantian Liberal Peace (Revisited)', *American Journal of Political Science*, 51 (2) (2007), 397–414.

Duncombe, Stephen (ed.). *Cultural Resistance Reader* (London: Verso, 2002).

Eisenman, Stephen F. *The Abu Ghraib Effect* (London: Reaktion Books, 2007).

Frazer, Elizabeth and Kimberly Hutchings. *Can Political Violence Ever Be Justified?* (Cambridge: Polity Press, 2019).

Gunatilleke, Godfrey, Neelan Tiruchelvam and Radhika Coomarswamy. 'Violence and Development in Sri Lanka: Conceptual Issues', in Gunatilleke, Tiruchelvam and Coomarswamy (eds.), *Ethical Dilemmas of Development in Asia* (Lexington, MA: Lexington Books, 1983).

Hyams, Edward. *Killing No Murder* (London: Panther, 1970).

Hyman, James. *The Battle for Realism, Figurative Art in Britain during the Cold War 1945–60* (New Haven: Yale University Press, 2001).

Jones, Jonathan. 'Ai Weiwei Is Making a Feature Film: I'm Worried', *The Guardian*, 3 May 2016.

Juris, Jeffrey S. 'Violence Performed and Imagined: Militant Action, the Black Bloc and the Mass Media in Genoa', *Critique of Anthropology*, 25 (4) (2005), 313–432.

Kaplan, Robert D. 'The Anarchy that Came', *The National Interest*, October 2018, https://nationalinterest.org/feature/anarchy-came-33872 [last accessed 17 October 2019].

Kaplan, Robert D. 'The Coming Anarchy', *The Atlantic*, February 1994, www.theatlantic.com/magazine/archive/1994/02/the-coming-anarchy/304670/ [last accessed 17 October 2019].

Klingender, F.D. *Goya in the Democratic Tradition*, [orig. pub 1948] with Introduction by Herbert Read (London: Sidgwick & Jackson, 1968).

Kurant, Agnieszka, Sowa, Jan and Szadkowski, Krystian. 'Afterword: Do We Need a Lab? Capture, Exploitation and Resistance in Contemporary Creative Communities' in Michał Kozłowski, Agnieszka Kurant, Jan Sowa, Krystian Szadkowski, Jakub Szreder (eds.), *Joy Forever, Political Economy of Social Creativity* (London: MayFly Books, 2014), 249–58.

Lorde, Audre. *Sister Outsider: Essays and Speeches by Audre Lorde* (Berkeley: Crossing Press, 2007 [1984]).

Mbembe, Achille. *On the Postcolony* (Berkeley: University of California Press, 2001).

McQuiston, Liz. *Visual Impact, Creative Dissent in the 21st Century* (London: Phaidon, 2015).

Menke, Christoph. 'Law and Violence', in Gerrit Jackson (trans.), *Law and Violence: In Dialogue* (Manchester: Manchester University Press, 2018), 3–75.

Minor Compositions. *A User's Guide to (Demanding) the Impossible* (Wivenhoe, New York and Port Watsons: Autonomedia, n.d.).

Mitchell, W.J.T. 'The Violence of Public Art: Do the Right Thing', *Critical Inquiry*, 16 (1990), 880–99.

Mouffe, Chantal. 'Artistic Activism and Agonistic Spaces', *Art and Research: A Journal of Ideas, Contexts and Methods*, 1 (2) (2007), 1–5.

O'Neill, Brendan. 'The Orlando Massacre and the Crisis of Humanism', *Spiked*, 16 June 2016, www.spiked-online.com/newsite/article/the-orlando-massacre-and-the-crisis-of-humanism/18452#.V45aofkrK71

Parker, Martin. 'Eating with the Mafia: Belonging and Violence', *Human Relations*, 61 (7) (2008), 989–1006.

Popovic Sroja. *Blueprint for Revolution: How to Use Rice Pudding, Lego Men and Other Non-violent Techniques to Galvanise Communities, Overthrow Dicators, or Simply Change the World* (Victoria, Australia and London: Scribe, 2015).

Reclus, Elie. *Primitive Folk: Studies in Comparative Ethnology* (London: Walter Scott, n.d.).

Shapiro, Michael J. *Studies in Trans-Disciplinary Method: After the Aesthetic Turn* (Abingdon: Routledge, 2013).

Schneider, Jane and Peter Schneider. 'Mafia, Antimafia, and the Question of Sicilian Culture', *Politics & Society*, 22 (2) (1994), 237–58.

Schoenberger, Erica. 'Interdiscilinarity and Social Power', *Progress in Human Geography*, 25 (3) (2001), 365–82.

Stevens, Quentin, Franck, Karen and Fazakerley, Ruth. 'Counter-monuments: the Anti-monumental and the Dialogic', *The Journal of Architecture*, 17 (2012), 951–72.

Stewart, Pamela J. and Andrew Strathern. *Violence: Theory and Ethnography* (New York and London: Continuum, 2002).

Stitt, André. *Small Time Life* (London: Black Dog Publishing, 2001).

Strathern, Andrew and Pamela J. Stewart. 'Introduction: Terror, the Imagination, and Cosmology', in Stratern, Stewart and Neil L. Whitehead (eds.), *Terror and Violence* (London: Pluto, 2006), 1–39.

Unger, Clio. '"SHOOT HIM NOW!!!" Anonymity, Accountability and Online Spectatorship in Wafaa Bilal's Domestic Tension', *International Journal of Performance Arts and Digital Media*, 11 (2015), 202–18.

Ursprung, Philip. 'More Than the Art World Can Tolerate, Otto Muehl's Mano-psychotic Ballet', *Tate etc*, 25 June 2019, www.tate.org.uk/tate-etc/issue-15-spring-2009/more-art-world-can-tolerate [last accessed 20 November 2019].

Weiner, Andrew Stefan. 'Reevaluating Actionism: Austrian Performance, Then and Now', *PAJ: A Journal of Performance and Art*, 37 (3) (2015), 50–7.

Whiteley, Gillian. '"Sewing the Subversive Thread of Imagination": Jeff Nuttall, Bomb Culture and the Radical Potential of Affect', *The Sixties, A Journal of History, Politics and Culture*, 4 (2) (December 2011), 109–33.

Williams, Sam. Stuart Brisley, *Aesthetica*, 36, February 2015, https://aestheticamagazine.com/stuart-brisley/ [last accessed 2 March 2020].

Žižek, Slovoj, *Violence* (London: Profile Books, 2009).

1 From Watts to Wall Street

A Situationist analysis of political violence

Martin Lang

Introduction

This chapter approaches the theme of political violence through a Situationist lens. The Situationist International (SI) were highly political artists that could be considered proto art activists, if not art activists proper. The focus of the first part of the chapter will be their essay 'The Decline and Fall of the Spectacle Commodity Economy' – first published in the tenth issue of the Situationists' eponymous journal *Internationale Situationiste* on 10 March 1966,[1] seven months after the Watts Rebellion (Los Angeles, 1965) that it analyses.[2] The chapter is, then, from the outset concerned with artists' interpretations of, as well as opinions and influences on, political violence.

'The Decline and Fall . . .' has received little critical attention. Only Heath Schultz's recent article addresses the SI text in depth (Schultz, 2018). Schultz contrasts Debord's 'Marxism' with Afropessimism, ultimately to show that the two positions are not as unreconcilable as they first appear. He does this, largely, through an analysis of imagery of the Watts Rebellion in Debord's film version of *Society of the Spectacle* (1973).

Gavin Grindon dedicates a section of his 2015 essay on what he calls the Situationists' 'fantasy of brainwashed political violence' to their assessment of Watts. Like Shultz, he focuses on their use of imagery (from Watts) and accuses them of not engaging with Watts directly but through 'the spectacle of Watts projected across the media' (Grindon, 2015b: 79). While Grindon recognises 'riot' as 'an open legal category blanketing a variety of particular forms of mass-cultural public assembly as "disorder"', he nonetheless describes Watts as 'a black working class riot' (Grindon, 2015b: 79). Grindon's verdict is that the SI's assessment of Watts is to fetishise its political violence, rather than recognise the potential of the riot-as-festival. Although Grindon is critical, 'The Decline and Fall . . .' is not the main focus of his essay: it is not mentioned until after seventeen pages.

The first major study on the SI – Sadie Plant's *The Most Radical Gesture* (first published in 1992) – only mentions 'The Decline and Fall . . .' once. Plant claims that it deals with a situation that has 'since reasserted itself in countless instances from Handsworth to Brixton' (2002: 30). Plant likens the SI assessment that Watts was a commodity 'riot' to the Poll Tax riots (UK, 1990), in which she claims emblems of consumption were attacked – 'the most expensive shops, the brightest neon signs, and the most prestigious cars' (2002: 31). The Situationist claim – that the unrest of 1965 was a rebellion against the commodity economy, not a 'race riot' – will be the central contention of this chapter.[3]

Other books on the SI similarly pay short shrift to their assessment of the Watts Rebellion. McKenzie Wark does not mention the essay in *The Spectacle of Disintegration* (2013), although she does mention Watts in passing. Simon Sadler's *The Situationist City* (1998) does not mention it either, although he includes an illustration on page 162.

In *Beneath the Beach the Street* (first published 2011), Wark dedicates nearly a couple of pages to 'The Decline and Fall . . .'. She partly agrees with the SI assessment that the Watts Rebellion was a revolt against the commodity – concurring that Black Americans were able to see through the spectacle. She also considers Watts as a 'cruel reminder of inequity to Black America' (Wark, 2015: 148). Wark notes that the SI account omitted many details: 'the thirty dead, the thousands injured, the four thousand arrests' (2015: 148). However, it is uncertain how much attention she really gives the matter, since she incorrectly claims, 'Before Watts, there was Newark, July that same year' (2015: 147) – in fact the riots in Newark took place two years later in July 1967.

Building on these accounts, this chapter will include a substantial analysis of Situationists' account of Watts, subjecting their claims to scrutiny by comparing them to other historical sources, such as government inquiries and newspaper reports – both contemporary to the events and looking back on various anniversaries and milestones.

The second text that I refer to in the first part of this chapter is Black Mask's account of the Newark 'riots', published in the seventh issue of their eponymous newspaper (1967). Black Mask were certainly art activists and might also be considered the SI's New York wing. Gavin Grindon writes that they were 'excluded from the Situationist International without having ever agreed to join' (2015a: 186). According to Grindon, Black Mask were in contact with the 'English Situationists' (T.J. Clark, Donald Nicholson Smith, Charles Radcliffe, Dave and Stuart Wise), and leading Belgian Situationist Raoul Vaneigem 'travelled to New York to visit potential situationists there, but refused to meet Morea' (2015a: 185–6).[4] When the English Situationists protested Black Mask's exclusion, they too were expelled (Grindon, 2015: 186). Grindon draws parallels between the expulsion of Surrealists and Black Mask's situation – terming them 'dissident Situationists' (2015a: 187).

The originality of the second part of the chapter will lie in its application of the Situationist analyses of political violence in the 1960s to more contemporary iterations. It will highlight similarities between the Situationists' assessment of the Watts Rebellion, Black Mask's account of the Newark riots and the 'August riots' of 2011.[5] The aim, as will become clear, is to question whether the 'long, hot summer of 1967'[6] and the 'European Summer' of 2011 played comparable roles as precursors to the occupations that came shortly after (May '68/Occupy).[7] The second part also applies the Situationist analysis of Watts to Occupy, highlighting its moralistic and individualistic ethos to make surprising links with earlier claims about race and class. Then, investigation into recent scholarship on race and class will inform my final assessment of the Situationist claims made in 'The Decline and Fall of the Spectacle-Commodity Economy' and whether they remain relevant today.

The Watts Rebellion and the long, hot summer of 1967

In the aftermath of the protests, occupations and riots of May '68, Situationist René Viénet claimed that 'the commodity system was undoubtedly the target of the aggressiveness shown by the masses' (2014: §6).[8] He quotes de Gaulle's televised speech of 7 June 1968, in which the French president also acknowledged that 'this explosion was provoked by groups in revolt against modern consumer and technical society' (Viénet, 2014: §8). Viénet notes that:

> The situationists had foreseen for years that the permanent incitement to accumulate the most diverse objects, in exchange for the insidious counterpart of money, would one day provoke the anger of masses abused and treated as consumption machines.
>
> (2014: §6)

Indeed, the SI did foresee a build-up of mass dissatisfaction with consumer capitalism: not in France but in the United States. They took a keen interest in US race relations and civil unrest, imagining the Watts Rebellion as the first stage in a broader struggle, signs of which they saw in the 1964 student strike at University of Berkeley that was linked to both civil rights and the Vietnam War. They predicted that African Americans had the potential to 'unmask the contradictions of the most advanced capitalist system' (Situationist International, 2006: 195). In the obituary of 'the man who started the [Watts] riot', the *New York Times* described the Watts Rebellion as the biggest insurrection by African Americans in the United States since the slave revolts (25 December 1986). The uprising in Watts was the catalyst for a series of riots across America (1965–67) that I refer to as the 'long, hot summers'.[9]

At first, it seemed obvious that the Watts 'riots' were 'race riots', as they were described as such in the *Los Angeles Times*. For example, on 13 August they reported that an eighteen-year-old girl admitted to throwing bricks and rocks at 'anything white' (Hillinger and Jones, 1965). The *LA Times* also reported on how the riots were perceived abroad. It was front-page news in several countries, including the UK and South Africa. On 15 August, under the headline 'Reds Call L.A. Rioting Evidence of Race Bias', they reported that the foreign communist press was taking the opportunity to highlight US discontent (Associated Press, 1965). The New China News Agency is reported to have said that the riot was evidence of 'a general outburst of their (negroes) pent-up dissatisfaction' – the brackets, we assume, were inserted by the *LA Times*.

Contemporary reports from the *LA Times* did refer to racial tensions, but headlines also referred to 'negro heroism' saving whites (13 August 1965). Referring to sociologists' and other expert opinions, mixed reasons were reported for the rioting (on 14 and 17 August) and even doubts that 'racial hostility' was the cause of the riots at all (14 August). The SI went further, declaring that 'The Watts riot was not a *racial* conflict' (Situationist International, 2006: 196). Instead, they claimed that what they were witnessing was a 'rebellion against the commodity . . . in which worker-consumers are hierarchically subordinated to commodity standards' (2006: 197).

The SI proclaimed that looters targeted 'black shops' and left 'whites' alone, only targeting white police officers. Similarly, their analysis of 'black-on-black' crimes is used as evidence that Watts was not a race riot: 'black solidarity did not extend to black store-owners or even to black car-drivers' (Situationist International, 2006: 196). Their estimation of events is contradicted by some news reports. For example, a reporter for the *Los Angeles Sentinel* (the principal paper serving the black community at the time) reported that 'the problem, as far as the residents were concerned, is that they were white-owned stores, selling substandard stuff for high prices' (Landsberg and Reitman, 2005). The *Sentinel* also reported how a large supermarket, notorious for bad quality food, was burned to the ground, without even being looted, while a tiny grocery store was left untouched because it was black-owned.

The *Sentinel* and some of the reports in the *LA Times* seem to cast doubt on the SI account. Were the SI unfairly attributing a revolt against consumer capitalism to a series of incidents on the other side of the world that they could not comprehend? Or, could it be that they were right? Might we consider that the supermarket owners happened to be white but also represented a ruling elite that owned property in a working-class neighbourhood?

The SI were not alone in their assessment. We have already seen that popular accounts were conflicted regarding the cause of the 'riots', but there is also testimony from more authoritative sources. Two days after the unrest ended, Martin Luther King visited Watts and subsequently declared that the causes were

> environmental and not racial. The economic deprivation, social isolation, inadequate housing, and general despair of thousands of Negroes teeming in Northern and Western ghettos are the ready seeds which give birth to tragic expressions of violence.
>
> (https://kinginstitute.stanford.edu)

As is customary following riots, an inquiry was set up to establish the cause. The McCone Commission's report recommended, among other things: '"emergency" literacy and preschool programs, improved police-community ties, increased low-income housing, more job-training projects, upgraded health-care services, more efficient public transportation' – although on the twenty-fifth anniversary of the riots the *LA Times* reported that most of these measures were never implemented (Dawsey, 1990).

The SI declared that one reason the unrest was more likely in LA than other US cities was relative poverty. African Americans in LA, they tell us, were wealthier than the average African American, but they were also surrounded by the 'superopulence' of Hollywood 'that is flaunted all around them' (Situationist International, 2006: 198). Previous revolutions have encountered the problem of scarcity; the Watts Rebellion highlighted the problem of abundance. The SI recognised this when they noted that:

> Unable to believe in any significant chance of integration or promotion, the Los Angeles blacks take modern capitalist propaganda, its publicity of abundance, literally. They want to possess now all the objects shown and abstractly accessible, because they want to use them.
>
> (2006: 197)

One of the SI's examples of how the LA black community took the 'capitalist propaganda' literally is how they stole fridges. They were apparently seduced by their exchange value, even though they had no use value given that many of the looters either did not have electricity, or if they did, they could not afford to pay the bill (Situationist International, 2006: 197). This highlighted the myth of abundance for all. We are told that if we all work hard, we will all become rich, but this is impossible.

Dutch artist Renzo Martens' artwork *Institute for Human Activity* (2012–present) illustrates this predicament. He mocks such assumptions by setting up a cultural centre in a remote location in the Congolese jungle, on the site of a former Unilever palm oil plantation. When the palm oil extraction was exhausted, Unilever pulled out leaving mass unemployment. Martens invited Richard Florida, author of the influential book *The Rise of the Creative Class* (2002), to deliver a keynote speech via satellite phone at the centre's opening conference. He asked Florida if the lack of roads and infrastructure would impede the development of his art institute. Florida, oblivious to the irony, said that this would not be a problem: once the demand was created, supply would come. Speaking at a conference at Tate Modern,[10] Martens quipped that he was now waiting for the hipster cappuccino bars to spring up. Of course, this is impossible. Consumers can only afford hipster coffee because of economic inequality. By taking this logic of abundance literally, Martens exposes its impossibility. Likewise, the African American looters in Watts pointed to the fact that consumerism necessitates economic exploitation: mainly black Americans in America 1965, the Congolese and the Global South more generally in the globalised economies of 2018.

The Los Angeles black community was demanding unfettered access to the spectacle-commodity economy on equal terms to the white community. However, the SI claim it is 'the nature of the spectacle that it cannot be actualized either immediately or equally, *not even for the whites*' (2006: 200, emphasis in original). Inequality, in their view, is a necessary condition of the spectacle-commodity economy, and adherence to its logic was encouraged through the symbol of the African American, who illustrated 'the threat of falling into such wretchedness' to spur 'others on in the rat-race' (Situationist International, 2006: 200).

'The Decline and Fall . . .' is a conflicted article. Although the SI clearly assert that the Watts Rebellion was not a racial conflict and although their analysis of the causes points to social and economic reasons, they do acknowledge the racial divide:

> Just as the human riches of the American blacks are despised and treated as criminal, monetary riches will never make them completely acceptable in America's alienated society: individual wealth will only make a rich nigger because blacks as a whole must represent poverty in a society of hierarchized wealth.
>
> (Situationist International, 2006: 198)

They also recognised that until 1959 many Los Angeles unions refused to accept African Americans as members. However, it is here that they make an interesting, if controversial, observation. The SI argued that the black community represented a radical potential for negating the commodity system, *precisely because* they had not yet been integrated into it and that racial equality would only mean integration into the spectacle-commodity economy – 'the blacks are the rallying point for all those who refuse the logic of this integration into capitalism, which is all that the promise of racial integration amounts to' (Situationist International, 2006: 200).

The SI supported and defended the Watt rebels; indeed, it has been said that the Situationists were the only 'whites' at the time to defend the rioting black community and to fully grasp the revolutionary feeling coming to the boil (Gray, 2001: 3). They declared that, because of their lack of integration, African Americans could 'see more quickly through the falsehood of the whole economic-cultural spectacle' (2006: 200). At the same time, they delivered a warning about ignoring the broader systemic conditions of oppression – 'the spectacle-commodity economy'.

This is perhaps one reason for the wave of African American uprisings that spread across America in the wake of the Watts Rebellion that became known as the 'long, hot summer of 1967'.[11] In total, there were 159 riots in several major US cities. The most serious occurred in Newark and Detroit.[12] Following the Detroit riots, President Johnson established an inquiry, headed by the Kerner Commission. The report (1968) noted that:

> What the rioters appeared to be seeking was fuller participation in the social order and the material benefits enjoyed by the majority of American citizens. Rather than rejecting the American system, they were anxious to obtain a place for themselves in it.
>
> (The National Advisory Commission on
> Civil Disorders, 2016: 7)

Both the Kerner report and the SI account highlight the role that economic, material conditions played in the festering sense of dissatisfaction in the US black communities. Both accounts emphasise that the American black communities aspired to have the commodities that they were unable to own. Rather than seeing this as an endorsement of the commodity economy (as the Kerner report does), the SI saw a radical potential to undermine it. As we have already seen, the black community revealed the impossibility of abundance for all by demanding their equal share. The SI expand that:

> In taking the capitalist spectacle at its face value, the blacks are already rejecting the spectacle itself. The spectacle is a drug for slaves. It is designed not to be taken literally, but to be followed from just out of reach; when this separation is eliminated, the hoax is revealed.
>
> (Situationist International, 2006: 200)

In August 1967, the anarchist art collective Black Mask published the seventh edition of their eponymous newspaper.[13] In this issue they quoted two accounts of the 1967 Newark riots. The first is taken from the *New York Times* (16 July 1967): 'At times, amidst the scenes of riot and destruction that made parts of the city look like a battlefield, there was an almost carnival atmosphere' (Hahne and Morea, 2011: 46). The second is from *Time* magazine (21 July 1967): 'Said [New Jersey] Governor Hughes after a tour of the riot-blighted streets. . . . "The thing that repelled me most was the holiday atmosphere. . . . It's like laughing at a funeral"' (Hahne and Morea, 2011: 47).

'Yes!' Black Mask agree:

> We laugh at this funeral. . . . [Governor Hughes] belongs to an obsolete generation, the last of a system at whose burial we cannot but burst in joy . . . he is only repelled by their enjoyment, their holiday atmosphere, as soon as they transcend the commodity enslavement and so do [sic] transcend him.
>
> (Hahne and Morea, 2011: 47)

Then, Black Mask makes a claim that also points to systemic causes rather than racially aggravated ones:

> Sure 'they don't hate so much the white man as they do hate America,' America as it is abused and dominated by a handful of white, clean washed, cool blooded gangsters. In their disgust of this America the Black Man does not stay alone!
>
> (Hahne and Morea, 2011: 47)

The two media reports of the Newark riots that describe a carnival or holiday atmosphere could easily be recounting the 2011 August riots. There are other similarities between the 'long, hot summer' and the 'European Summer' of 2011 that I will explore through a Situationist-style analysis of the August riots in the second part of this chapter.

The European Summer and Occupy

Mark Duggan, a twenty-nine-year-old British man of mixed race, was shot dead by the Metropolitan Police in North London on 4 August 2011. Two days after Duggan's death, his family – many of whom are West Indian – along with residents from the Broadwater Farm estate, marched on Tottenham Police Station demanding answers.[14] Initially the protests were peaceful. Accounts of what happened next vary, but some claim a teenage girl threw something and was promptly set upon by police with batons and shields (Beckford and Gardham, 2011; Lewis, 2011). The crowd responded by burning police cars. The protests spread across Tottenham, one of the capital's most ethnically diverse areas. It is easy to see how this looked like a racially aggravated protest about police brutality against Mark Duggan and, by proxy, the black community. I am not arguing that it was not, but the looting that followed across the city, then across England,[15] had little to do with race and, as in LA 1965, everything to do with commodities.

Writing while the riots were still underway, Alain Badiou noted how David Cameron categorised the looters as mere hoodlums, contrasting them with the 'good citizens' whose property needs defending (2012: 16). Cameron simultaneously announced new tough measures to deal with the 'hooligans', using laws established under the Blair government with the result that the UK 'has many more prisoners as a percentage of its population than France, which does not pull any punches when it comes to locking up youth' (Badiou, 2012: 16). Badiou notes how the full force of the law was televised. Images of riot police smashing through the front doors of suspects denounced by 'good citizens', he claims, shows that the state does not give a damn about the property of the poor (2012: 17). At the same time, Badiou notes the 'infinite tolerance for the crimes of bankers and government embezzlers which affect the lives of millions' (2012: 19).

Comparing the situation in London to the unrest in France (2005), Badiou notes that the 'spark that "lights a prairie fire" is always a state murder', usually of a 'Black hooligan' or Arab 'known to the police' (2012: 18). Apparently, 'the destruction or theft of a few goods in the frenzy of a riot is infinitely more culpable than the police assassination of a young man' (Badiou, 2012: 19). While Badiou recognises the racial element or spark, he is clear to couch the overall riot in terms of Marx's theory of alienation, noting 'the primacy of things over existence, of commodities over life and machines over workers' (2012: 20).

The UK government commissioned an independent Riots, Communities and Victims Panel to investigate the causes behind the rioting. The report showed that local communities and victims shared 'concerns about brands and materialism'. One of the six 'key areas' set out in the report is entitled 'riots and the brands' (Marcus et al., 2012: 6) – this section features seven separate recommendations. The panel found that 85 per cent of people feel advertising puts pressure on young people to own the latest products and nearly 70 per cent felt that materialism was a problem and that measures were needed to decrease the amount of advertising directed at young people (Marcus et al., 2012: 10).

The fact that looters targeted brands (rather than non-branded commodities) also suggests that advertising played a role in their motivation. Just as the Situationists and the McCone Commission concluded about the Watts Rebellion, the UK government-appointed independent panel reasoned that it was consumer culture (not race relations) that underlay the riots. This deduction seems plausible: anybody who watched the news footage will have noticed that there were at least as many white people involved in the rioting and looting. People from varied backgrounds and of varied ages, incidentally, took trainers and sweets with the same zeal as when they took plasma screen televisions. Like the Los Angeles black community, British youths had been told they needed to have certain commodities, so when the opportunity arose . . . they took them.

Both government reports describe an underlying spirit fraught with consumerist issues, but could it be coincidental that commodity riots, with a carnival or holiday atmosphere, preceded both May '68 and Occupy in 2011? First, I will argue that the SI attempted to harness the tensions they perceived in Watts and release them in the events of May '68. Then I will argue that there is a similar link between the August riots and Occupy.

The SI were well-known to have influenced, maybe even instigated, the events of May '68 (Wollen, 1989: 67, 71; Lasn, 2000: xvi, 213; Gallix, 2009; Kurczynski, 2010; Knabb, 2011; McKee, 2016). They were involved in the occupations from the beginning, and it was they who made two key demands: to maintain direct democracy in the assembly and that workers across the whole country occupy their factories and form workers' councils (Knabb, 2011). Furthermore, the assembly could be understood in terms of Raoul Vaneigem's call for open dialogue and the distribution and simplification of information, published just the year before (Vaneigem, 2001: 103). The SI were also involved with the Atelier Populaire, established in the occupied lithography studios of the Paris École des Beaux-Arts, where they produced political posters and enigmatic slogans – the sheer amount produced suggests that many people were involved (Considine, 2015). In 1966, 'On the Poverty of Student Life' was written and circulated by the SI and students of the University of Strasbourg. The pamphlet was re-issued and widely distributed at the Nanterre campus in May 1967 (Dark Star, 2001: 6). The two seminal Situationist texts, *The Society of the Spectacle* (Debord) and *The Revolution of Everyday Life* (Vaneigem), were both published later that year. So, without becoming embroiled in a debate about who contributed more to the build-up to the occupations and riots of May 1968, we can at least assert that the SI played an influential role.

In the same year they were co-authoring political pamphlets with students in France, the SI also published 'The Decline and Fall of the Spectacle-Commodity Economy', which also mentions the Algerian Revolution and appears in issue ten of *Situationiste Internationale* alongside three articles on the unrest in Algeria.[16] This suggests they were thinking globally. I have already established that they considered African American revolt as a kind of precursor of something to come. According to Viénet, they had already identified, before May '68, that incitement to accumulate 'would one day provoke the anger of masses abused and treated as consumption machines' (2014: §6). The evidence suggests that the SI were thinking about these things together. It is therefore fair to speculate that they recognised the global potential of anti-commodity sentiment in Watts and later attempted to release it in France.

We have seen that the Watts Rebellion and the unrest of the 'long, hot summer of 1967' received significant press coverage abroad, even making the international front pages. Furthermore, the SI account of Watts was one of their most 'readily available in the late sixties' (Dark Star, 2001: 6). It is therefore fair to assume that the occupiers in Paris were aware of these 'riots'. Even if only on a subconscious level, they would have been able to tap into a growing sense of dissatisfaction, rage even, against consumer capitalism.

To declare that the August riots influenced Occupy in a comparable fashion is less straightforward. There is no equivalent analysis by artists (such as the SI) of the August riots, but the earlier accounts by Badiou and the UK government panel, when seen in terms of the Situationist analysis of Watts, reveal similarities. Occupy has been considered as building on the Arab Spring (2010–12) and a 'European Summer' of riots and occupations.[17] Others have also linked the political violence in North Africa to the unrest that followed in Europe (see, for example, Badiou, 2012; Eggert, 2011). This reminds us that both the occupations of May '68 and Occupy were preceded by riots but also by unrest in North Africa. The Arab Spring, first in Tunisia, then Egypt and Libya, recalls the Algerian Revolution (1954–62) that so fascinated the SI. These historical similarities and Thompson's chronology suggest that the 'European Summer' affected or maybe helped to form the Occupy movement.

To declare that the SI influenced Occupy is not clear-cut, since they disbanded in 1972. However, there is evidence to support the claim that their ideas influenced its formation. The July 2011 issue of *Adbusters* magazine featured an advertisement that was the original call for people to 'Occupy Wall Street': it read: '#OCCUPYWALLSTREET. September 17th. Bring tent. www.occupywallst.org' (Elliott, 2011).

Adbusters describe themselves as an 'international collective of artists, designers, poets, punks, writers, directors, musicians, philosophers, drop outs, and wild hearts' (www.adbusters.org/). They were not only key to the foundation of Occupy; they are also overtly and heavily linked to Situationist theory and tactics. For example, their blend of modern advertising techniques with irony, collage and pastiche echoes the Situationists' subversive elements and tactics. Adbusters' editor and co-founder Kalle Lasn draws parallels between Situationist détournement and its contemporary variants in his books *Culture Jam* (2000), *Design Anarchy* (2006) and *Meme Wars* (2012). While not proof that Situationist theory influenced the Occupy movement, it does show us that a key organiser was familiar with and influenced by the Situationists.

David Graeber was another early, key figure in the Occupy movement. In 2011, *Rolling Stone* magazine credited Graeber with giving the Occupy movement its slogan 'we are the 99%' (Sharlet, 2011), although others claim it appeared on an anonymous blog first. Graeber is similarly familiar with Situationism. He wrote about the SI's role in the build-up to May '68 in his book *Direct Action* (2009), asserting that their thought was influential on the Global Justice Movement. Graeber notes that, while academics have focussed on the writers that emerged after 1968, such as 'Deleuze, Foucault or Baudrillard', who reflected on what went wrong and concluded that revolutionary dreams are impossible, punks and revolutionaries are still reading 'theory from immediately before '68' (2009: 259). Graeber asserts that two strains of French thought emerged from 1968: the pre-'68 strain 'kept alive in zines, anarchist infoshops, and the Internet' (the SI falls into this category) and the post-'68 strain that exists in academia (Graeber, 2009: 259–60). He notes:

> The Situationists argued that the system renders us passive consumers, but issued a call to actively resist. The current radical academic orthodoxy seems to reject either the first part or the second: that is, either it argues that there is no system imposed on consumers, or that resistance is impossible.
>
> (Graeber, 2009: 260)

Graeber mentions the SI on fourteen pages in this book alone. Therefore, there is evidence that more than one of the key Occupy organisers was at least aware of and probably influenced by the SI.

The effect that artists had on Occupy was not limited to Adbusters' and Graeber's mediation of Situationist thought. Yates McKee has argued that Occupy was a movement with artists at its core from the very beginning: not as illustrators of the movement but as fundamental components to its planning and organisation (McKee, 2017). McKee describes how curator Nato Thompson ended his closing remarks at the Creative Time Summit by urging the attendees to 'visit a little-known plaza in the financial district called Zuccotti Park', which had, for the past week, been 'the staging ground for something hazily known as "Occupy Wall Street"' (McKee, 2016).

The general assembly that prefigured the Occupy Wall Street camp, McKee explains, was:

> launched from a para-artistic space (16 Beaver) and held at an aesthetically charged site (Charging Bull, reframed by the Adbusters poster)... it was inaugurated with a call from an artist [Georgia Sagri] to desert the representational space of the stage, with its special hierarchy of speaker and audience, its dependence on official state permission.
>
> (2016)

For McKee, the artists involved in Occupy embodied the indebted, precarious workers on zero hours contracts that emerged in such large numbers after the banking crisis of 2008. They differ from the artists involved in May '68 in this regard and because many of them came from a generation raised to believe that being an artist was akin to being an entrepreneur: that if they just worked harder they could grasp the American dream. Occupy was the moment when this illusion was rejected. At least some of these artists were familiar with Situationist thought. For example, Ayreen Anastas and Rene Gabri had previously undertaken a summer-long psychogeographical détournement of the road trip to 'test out Agamben's thesis that "the camp is the nomos of the modern" considering their own question, "How can a camp like Guantanamo exist in our own time?"' (McKee, 2016).

Having established similarities between the 'long, hot summer of 1967' and the August 2011 riots and links between Situationism and Occupy, let us return to my claim that Occupy was – to some degree – formed by the political violence of the 'European Summer'. Returning to Badiou's theory of the riot gives us another means to claim a connection. For Badiou, the August riots are an example of an 'immediate riot'. Immediate riots start at the location of the 'spark', usually following state violence or provocation. These riots may spread by imitation, but they will still be 'immediate': they will continue to stagnate in their own social spaces as they rage upon themselves, attack symbols of wealth, 'particularly cars, shops and banks', and 'symbols of the state' (Badiou, 2012: 23). Often accused of destroying what little they have, immediate rioters demonstrate that 'when something is one of the few "benefits" granted you, it becomes the symbol not of its particular function, but of the general scarcity' (Badiou, 2012: 24).

For Badiou, when an immediate riot constructs a new site (usually in the city centre – Tahrir Square is his main example) 'where it endures and is extended, [then] it changes into an historical riot' (2012: 23). If we think globally, this transition could be mapped onto the August riots and Occupy. It is not clear that Badiou considers Occupy a 'historical riot' since it apparently lacks an 'Idea' (Badiou, 2012: 21). What is clear is that, for Badiou, immediate riots are often precursors to their historical variants (Badiou, 2012: 22).[18]

Graeber was aware of the August riots, as he was living in London at the time. His knowledge of Situationism allows us to speculate that he might have seen in the 'European Summer' a similar revolutionary anti-commodity potential that the SI saw in Watts. The SI urged us to see the structural conditions responsible for civil unrest. The accounts of the August riots by Badiou and the Riots, Communities and Victims Panel are commensurate with a Situationist analysis. Could such an analysis work with Occupy?

Wark's assessment of the 'The Decline and Fall . . .' that I mentioned in the introduction links Watts to Wall Street. Wark claims that although the Watts political unrest was leaderless, it was not without organisation – referring to the impromptu nightly meetings that took place in the park to coordinate events. She describes how gangs organised 'safe-conduct hand signals' that allowed members to stray outside their own patches (Wark, 2015: 148). This recalls the organisation of the Occupy movement, with their leaderless structure, hand signals, human microphones and so on. Occupy's focus on structure and organisation at the expense of an 'Idea', for Badiou, would undermine its potential development into a truly political 'historical riot'.

Writing in *FIELD: A Journal for Socially Engaged Art Criticism*, Sebastian Loewe identifies a moralistic element in Occupy's central claim that 'we are the 99%'. For Loewe, this is a fundamental flaw to its logic (2015: 187). By attributing the banking crisis to immoral behaviour, 'the 1%' are conceptualised as other – greedy bankers, for example. Such behaviour might be immoral, but, in most cases, they did nothing illegal. In fact, the system encouraged and rewarded risky investments with large bonuses. 'Stringing up' the bankers, like achieving racial equality, will not strike at the spectacle-commodity economy. Herein lies the similarity between the SI account of Watts and Loewe's assessment of Occupy.

More people joining the Occupy movement was considered evidence that the movement truly represented the 99% and that all grievances must be attributable to the 1%. As McKee notes:

> The ongoing ramifications of Occupy are evident across the spectrum of the Left, ranging from the invocation of the '1 percent' as a general class enemy in the self-described democratic socialist campaign of Bernie Sanders, to the rich debates concerning questions such as the party-form, communization, and platform cooperativism in contemporary theory – all of which have been recoded and radicalized by the emergence of Black Lives Matter.
>
> (McKee, 2016: Footnote 1)

This polyvocal 'movement' had to represent multiple grievances directed at various individuals who were all guilty of different moral crimes depending on each accuser's viewpoint. The ethos of Occupy was such that every voice must be given equal respect, while at the same time discouraging conflict. Loewe's analysis reminds us that such an inclusive polyvocal makeup renders each voice equally lost in a cacophony. Individuals might feel they are heard, but their opinion is also diluted. However, the polyvocal concerns manifested in Occupy should not simply be swept under the carpet. Let us focus on recent scholarship about race and class, since this is the issue that the SI tackled, and address arguments about their place in the assessment of recent civil unrest.

In *Class, Race and Marxism* (2017), David Roediger calls for thinking the politics of race and class together and bemoans that colour-blind politics has shifted to the Left. I will posit two examples that apply Roediger's refusal to side-line 'the consideration of race or, as in the case of liberal multiculturalism . . . questions of class' (Roediger, 2017: 6) to two related contemporary issues.

First, an example of how race has been side-lined in favour of class: Bernie Sanders has repeatedly claimed that class is more important than race and called for us to move beyond identity politics – one factor that has been attributed to his failed presidential campaign (Arceneaux, 2016). Sanders' position is compatible with the SI's account of Watts, but in an age of Black Lives Matter and #MeToo, is such a stance tenable?

A recent example of how identity politics ('liberal multiculturalism' in Roediger's terms) can side-line class unity can be found in the debates about whether Turner Prize nominee Luke Willis Thompson, a New Zealander of white and Fijian ancestry, has the right to make portraits about black people who have lost relatives to police brutality (Cascone, 2018; Cumming, 2018; Khong, 2018; Searle, 2018). This is the latest in a long list of controversies about cultural appropriation in art (see Malik, 2017). Recall, for example, Hannah Black's petition to have Dana Schutz's portrait of lynched black teenager Emmett Till (*Open Casket*, 2016) removed from the Whitney Biennial and destroyed (Charlesworth, 2017). The debate is whether white artists are profiting from making work about black suffering or, as others have argued, whether artists should be allowed to make work about whatever they like (Shaw, 2018).

Those outraged by apparent white appropriation of black suffering rarely pause to think that white artists can make work *in solidarity* with people of colour or that there are other factors that allow us to empathise with people of a different race. As Schutz argued: 'I don't know what it is like to be black in America but I do know what it is like to be a mother. . . . Their pain is your pain. My engagement with this image was through empathy with his mother' (Schutz in Charlesworth, 2017).

Like Schutz, Roediger points to the fact that we are more than our race. For example, he takes issue with David Harvey's claim that the unrest in Ferguson, Missouri (2014) had little to do with anticapitalism (Roediger, 2017: 1).[19] Roediger takes issue with what he perceives as Harvey's 'either or' approach. Roediger feels that the Ferguson unrest was an example of 'pro-worker struggles' aimed at ending the practice of 'shaking down the [neighbourhood's] working the poor' rather than 'taxing the large Emerson Electric corporation headquartered there' (Roediger, 2017: 2). Referring to Orlando de Guzman's film *Ferguson: Report from Occupied Territory* (2015), Roediger highlights an array of social issues that underpinned the Ferguson unrest: the abandoned neighbourhoods, derelict factories and unfair rents – *as well as* the racial tensions, especially with the police. Like the Situationists, he reconfigures what appears to be a race riot by considering multiple factors that influence political violence.

Roediger's case that Ferguson – and by implication the other 'riots' I have mentioned in this chapter – are about *both* race and class seems logical and appealing. However, he is attacking a 'straw man' in Harvey, who leaves the door open to intersectionality. While the *causes* might be economic and social as well as racial, Harvey's claim that *struggles* in Ferguson had little to do with anticapitalism could be true. Roediger criticises Harvey for claiming that Ferguson is part of a long history of preventing US racially aggravated unrest turning into wider social movements (Roediger, 2017: 1), but Harvey is not saying that Ferguson *should not* be anticapitalist or part of broader social movements. On the contrary, he warns that no struggles (racism and sexism, homophobia and so on) 'should transcend or supersede that against capital and its contradictions. Alliances of interests are clearly needed' (Harvey, 2014: 281). Harvey creates a hierarchy, but he avoids the pitfall of ranking race and class that Sanders fell into, by referring to 'anticapitalism'. The SI target the spectacle-commodity economy in much the same way.

While Harvey's claim that Ferguson was not an anticapitalist struggle does not prevent it becoming one, the Situationists' claim that 'The Watts riot was not a *racial* conflict' (2006: 196) shuts down the inverse possibility. So too did Martin Luther King, when he said that the causes were 'environmental and not racial' (https://kinginstitute.stanford.edu). This is the kind of binary thinking that Roediger opposes, and it is hard to deny that there were also racial elements in the 'long, hot summers'. Roediger's intersectional approach potentially bridges fragmentary identity politics (as seen in the critique of Thompson and Schutz), while Harvey reminds us that it is still possible to lose site of the bigger picture – struggles that are only about race and little to do with anticapitalism.

Conclusions

I draw two conclusions from this research. First, I conclude that both May '68 and Occupy were formed by the political violence that preceded them and that this relationship – between riot and occupation – illustrates Badiou's transition from 'immediate' to 'historical' riots.

Second, I conclude that, although the 'The Decline and Fall of the Spectacle-Commodity Economy' makes problematic and outmoded claims about race, the Situationist assessment of the spectacle-commodity economy provides a timely reminder to focus in solidarity on the bigger picture in the face of populism and nationalism. If combined with intersectional theory, it can also provide a counterbalance to identity politics, which can prevent the 'immediate' from becoming 'historical' by fragmenting mass social movements and undermining unity.

Notes

1 The essay is not signed, so I refer to it as being authored by the Situationist International throughout this chapter. However, the version on the Virginia Tech website states that it was written by their de facto leader Guy Debord, translated into English by Donald Nicholson-Smith and distributed in America in December 1965, just four months after the rebellion (see www.cddc.vt.edu). McKenzie Wark also attributes the article to Debord (2015: 148). All references and quotations in this chapter are taken from Ken Knabb's translation in the revised and expanded edition of his *Situationist International Anthology* (Knabb, 2006).

2 Also known as the 'Watts Riots', I refer to the political violence that erupted in Watts, Los Angeles (August 1965) as 'The Watts Rebellion'. This term has been used in encyclopaedic entries (https://kinginstitute.stanford.edu; www.black past.org), by universities (www.csudh.edu), political magazines such as the *Boston Review* (Franklin, 2015) and in academic journals (Murch, 2012). Donna Murch directly addresses the question of whether they were riots or a rebellion (2012: 37–9). She explains that 'the choice to use the term "riot" as opposed to "rebellion" reflected conflicting assumptions about the meaning not only of the popular street protests, but the larger significance of the historical period that immediately followed the passage of the 1965 Voting Rights Act' (2012: 37–8). For Murch, the term 'riot' embodies notions of spontaneity and destruction, while 'rebellions' are supposedly more planned and rational responses to legitimate grievances.

Recent scholarship on such violent civil unrest reclaims the term 'riot'. Joshua Clover's book *Riot. Strike. Riot* (2016) claims that 'riots' were the central form of protest until the nineteenth century when they were replaced by strikes, before the riot made a comeback in the 1970s. In *The Rebirth of History: Times of Riots and Uprisings* (2012), Alain Badiou discerns three types of 'riot': immediate, latent and historical. The first kind resembles Murch's 'riot': spontaneous, destructive, but failing to grow beyond its immediate location and time before petering out. The second kind resembles Clover's 'strike' but would also include other forms of mass actions such as demonstrations and blockades.

The 'historical riot' can be thought of as Murch's rebellion: it grows to include additional layers of people from various backgrounds, casting aside previously rigid social distinctions.

3 The fact the SI felt the need to deny that the Watts Rebellion was a race riot is noteworthy. Today, most encyclopaedic entries and popular accounts do not use the term 'race riot', although some do (www.npr.org; www.ranker.com). Nonetheless, despite not using the term 'race riot', most accounts imply that the Watts Rebellion was a series of racially motivated riots – even those sympathetic to the black cause. For example, on the fiftieth anniversary of the rebellion, Black Power in American Memory (a website maintained by the University of North Carolina) claimed that the spark for the unrest was 'racially charged abuse by the police' and refers to 'institutional racism' in the article title (http://black power.web.unc.edu). Luna Ray Films describes how in 1965 the Watts neighbourhood became the 'scene of the greatest example of racial tension America had seen' (www.pbs.org/). Blackpast.org claim that 'racial injustices' caused 'Watts' African American population to explode on August 11, 1965' (https://blackpast.org). The History Channel also refers to 'racial tension' as the cause of the riots (www.history.com). Whether or not the unrest in Watts 1965 were 'riots' and whether or not the unrest was 'racially motivated' will be critiqued throughout the first part of this chapter.

4 Ben Morea was the de facto leader of Black Mask.

5 Also referred to as the 'London riots' or the '2011 England riots', I use the UK government's preferred term (see Morrell et al., 2011; Marcus et al., 2012).

6 The 'long, hot summer of 1967' refers to 159 'riots' across the USA during the summer of 1967. It has been referred to by this name since the summer of 1967 in newspaper reports (see for example, *New York Times* 30 April 1967; 16 July 1967). It continues to be referred to by this name in the popular press (Gonsalves, 2017), in research contexts (Weldon, 2017) and in encyclopaedias (www. britannica.com).

It is also used as the title of a book by Malcolm McLaughlin – *The Long, Hot Summer of 1967: Urban Rebellion in America* (2014). McLaughlin tells us that newspapers referred to the 'long, hot summer' so often that it 'became almost a mantra in the press' (2014: 2). McLaughlin claims that the term dates to 1958, 'when it was chosen as the title of a film' (2014: 2). Although the film was not about the civil rights movement, McLaughlin feels it captured the tension in the South. It was in the 1960s, he tells us, that it became explicitly connected with civil rights. In 1964, Martin Luther King announced the start of a 'long, hot nonviolent summer' of protest (McLaughlin, 2014: 2).

7 The term 'European Summer' has been applied to the unrest preceding Occupy in a chronology referred to as the 'Arab Spring, European Summer and American Autumn' (Holloway, 2012: 199; Thompson, 2012: 32) or the 'Arab Spring, European Summer and American Fall' – this version being used on protest banners and as the title of a 2013 symposium whose papers were later re-printed in *Rethinking Marxism* (see The Editors, 2013: 146–51).

8 If the reader is interested in more details on the specific events of May 1968, I recommend Vladimir Fišera's documentary anthology published on the tenth anniversary (1978) or Anne Elletson's TV movie *Vive la Revolution!*, which was broadcast on the 50th anniversary (2018).

9 See endnote 6.

10 'The Politics of the Social in Contemporary Art', Friday 15 February 2013 (see www.tate.org.uk for more information).
11 See endnote 6.
12 The rioting in Detroit is the subject of Kathryn Bigelow's recent film *Detroit* (2017).
13 Black Mask went on to become the (even more) radical anarchist group Up Against the Wall Motherfucker! This name was allegedly taken from a poem titled 'Black People!' by the radical black poet Amiri Bakara, who participated in the Newark riots of 1967 (Grindon, 2015: 191). Bakara is referred to as a warrior poet. In issue six of *Black Mask,* Dan Georgakas likened him to the Watts rebels: 'Roi Jones [Amiri Bakara's birth name] and Watts guerrillas create kleftic cantos. As even in the poisonous cauldron of white America, the kleftic strain rises to war against Establishment and Spectacle. The warrior poet takes up his santouri and his weapons and the Junta understands full well' (Hahne and Morea, 2011: 43 [my brackets]). In 2014 Amiri's son Ras Bakara, was elected Mayor of Newark; he won re-election in 2018.
    The Outlaw Page, a leaflet written by John Sundstrom (a member of Up Against the Wall Motherfucker!) was used by the band Jefferson Airplane (almost verbatim) in the lyrics for their 1969 song 'We Can Be Together'. On 19 August 1969, the song was performed live on *The Dick Cavett Show* in what became known as 'the Woodstock show'. The song features the line 'In order to survive we steal, cheat, lie, forge, fuck, hide and deal', another reference to the ruthless competition of consumer capitalism. Since the performance was uncensored, it was also the first time the word 'fuck' had been uttered on US television – quickly followed by the phrase 'Up against the wall motherfucker' (Dangerous Minds, 2017). This points to how integrated the counter culture movement was: the phrase 'Up against the wall motherfucker' made its way from the Black Panthers, to a black poet, to an anarchist-Situationist collective and then onto US television via Jefferson Airplane.
14 To give some context, Duggan grew up on the Broadwater Farm estate, notorious for the 1985 race riot in which police officers were attacked and seriously injured, culminating in the death of PC Keith Blakelock. The last time a police officer was killed in a riot was in 1833 (Newman, 1986: 1), and only three officers have been killed in riots since the formation of the Metropolitan Police Force (Moore, 2015: 19). Timothy Brain's account of the murder cites eye witness fire officer Trevor Stratford, who described how forty to fifty people set upon Blakelock (Brain, 2010: 113). Tony Moore collates several testimonies that describe a mob carrying machetes, baseball bats and petrol bombs (Moore, 2015: 150, 152, 196, 207, 221). By the time Blakelock's body was recovered, he had sustained forty stab and slash wounds, his jaw was probably fractured by a machete and he had a knife buried into his neck up to the hilt (Brain, 2010: 113; McKillop, 1987: 3). The wound to his jaw was interpreted by the coroner as being consistent with an attempted beheading: a view backed up by witness statements that describe the intention to place Blakelock's head on a spike (McKillop, 1987: 3). Blakelock lost several fingers trying to defend himself (Moore, 2015: 152). The riots resulted in 186 arrests and eighty-four charges (Brain, 2010: 114).
15 The August riots were confined to English cities (London, Birmingham, Bristol, Gloucester, Gillingham, Liverpool, Manchester and Nottingham). They did not occur in Scotland, Wales or Northern Ireland.

16 These articles are translated as 'Address to Revolutionaries of Algeria and of All Countries', 'The Class Struggles in Algeria', and 'The Algeria of Daniel Guérin, Libertarian' in Ken Knabb's anthology (2006: 189–93, 203–12, 235–6).
17 See endnote 7.
18 For brief definitions of 'immediate' and 'historical' riots, see endnote 2.
19 Harvey is referring to the unrest following the murder of eighteen-year-old Mike Brown on 9 August 2014 (Ferguson, Missouri) in which more than 300 people were arrested.

Bibliography

Adbusters. 'Manifesto | Adbusters Media Foundation'. www.adbusters.org/manifesto.

Arceneaux, Michael. 'Bernie Sanders Still Says Class Is More Important than Race. He Is Still Wrong'. *The Guardian*, 22 November 2016. www.theguardian.com/commentisfree/2016/nov/22/bernie-sanders-identity-politics-class-race-debate.

Associated Press. 'Reds Call L.A. Rioting Evidence of Race Bias'. *Los Angeles Times*, 15 August 1965.

Badiou, Alain. *The Rebirth of History: Times of Riots and Uprisings* (Verso, 2012).

Beckford, Duncan and Martin Gardham. '"Attack" on Teenage Girl Blamed for Start of Tottenham Riot'. *Telegraph*, 8 August 2011. www.telegraph.co.uk/news/uknews/crime/8687547/Attack-on-teenage-girl-blamed-for-start-of-Tottenham-riot.html.

Bigelow, Kathryn. *Detroit* (Annapurna Pictures, 2017).

Brain, Timothy. *A History of Policing in England and Wales From 1974: A Turbulent Journey* (Oxford University Press, 2010).

Cascone, Sarah. '"Black Pain Is Not for Profit": An Activist Collective Protests Luke Willis Thompson's Turner Prize Nomination'. *artnet news*, 25 September 2018. https://news.artnet.com/exhibitions/luke-willis-thompson-turner-prize-1356151.

Charlesworth, J.J. 'On the Representation of People' (*ArtReview*, 69:3, 2017), 47.

Clover, Joshua. *Riot, Strike. Riot: The New Era of Uprisings* (Verso, 2016).

Considine, Liam. 'Screen Politics: Pop Art and the Atelier Populaire' (*Tate Papers*, 24, 2015). www.tate.org.uk/research/publications/tate-papers/24/screen-politics-pop-art-and-the-atelier-populaire.

CSUDH. 'The 1965 Watts Rebellion'. 2015. www.csudh.edu/watts/history/about/.

Cumming, Laura. 'Turner Prize 2018; Space Shifters Review – From the Momentous to the Miraculous'. *The Observer*, 30 September 2018. www.theguardian.com/artanddesign/2018/sep/30/turner-prize-2018-review-best-in-years-space-shifters-hayward-gallery.

Dangerous Minds. 'Grace Slick says "f*ck" on American TV for the Very First Time'. 2017. https://dangerousminds.net/comments/grace_slick_says_fck_on_american_tv_for_the_very_first_time_1969.

Dark Star, ed. *Beneath the Paving Stones: Situationists and the Beach, May 1968* (AK Press, 2001).

Dawsey, Darrell. '25 Years After the Watts Riots: McCone Commission's Recommendations Have Gone Unheeded'. *Los Angeles Times*, 8 July 1990. http://articles.latimes.com/1990-07-08/local/me-455_1_watts-riots.

Debord, Guy. 'The Decline and Fall of the Spectacle-Commodity Economy'. *Situationist International Online*. www.cddc.vt.edu/sionline/si/decline.html.

de Guzman, Orlando. *Ferguson: Report From Occupied Territory* (Fusion Media, 2015).

The Editors. 'Editors' Introduction' (*Rethinking Marxism*, 25:2, 2013), 146–51.

Eggert, Vanessa. 'From the Arab Spring to a European Summer' (*Democracy International*, 16 June 2011). www.democracy-international.org/arab-spring-european-summer.

Elletson, Anne. *Vive La Revolution! Joan Bakewell on May '68*. [TV Movie]. (Storyvault Films, BBC, 2018).

Elliott, Justin. 'The Origins of Occupy Wall Street Explained'. 2011. www.salon.com/2011/10/04/adbusters_occupy_wall_st/singleton/.

Encyclopaedia Britannica. 'The Riots of the Long, Hot Summer'. www.britannica.com/story/the-riots-of-the-long-hot-summer.

Fišera, Vladimir Claude. *Writing on the Wall, May 1968: A Documentary Anthology* (Allison & Busby, 1978).

Franklin, Sekou. 'Learning from the Watts Rebellion, 50 Years Later'. *Boston Review*, August 2015. http://bostonreview.net/us/sekou-franklin-watts-rebellion-50-years-later.

Gallix, Andrew. 'The Resurrection of Guy Debord'. *The Guardian*, 18 March 2009. www.theguardian.com/books/booksblog/2009/mar/18/guy-debord-situationist-international.

'The Ghetto Explodes in Another City'. *New York Times*, 16 July 1967, 131.

Gonsalves, Kelly. 'The "Long, Hot Summer of 1967"'. *The Week*, Summer 2017. http://theweek.com/captured/712838/long-hot-summer-1967.

Graeber, David. *Direct Action: An Ethnography* (AK Press, 2009).

Graeber, David. 'Revolution at the Level of Common Sense'. In Federico Campagna and Emanuele Campiglio, eds., *What We Are Fighting for: A Radical Collective Manifesto* (Pluto Press, 2012).

Gray, Chris. *Black Mask & Up Against the Wall Motherfucker: Burn It All Down: All You Need Is Dynamite: Flower Power Won't Stop Fascist Power: The Story of a Small, Underground 1960s Revolutionary Group in New York City* (The Daybreak Collective, 2001).

Grindon, Gavin. 'Fantasies of Participation: The Situationist Imaginary of New Forms of Labour in Art and Politics' (*The Nordic Journal of Aesthetics*, 24:49–50, 2015b), 62–90.

Grindon, Gavin. 'Poetry Written in Gasoline: Black Mask and Up Against the Wall Motherfucker' (*Art History*, 38:1, 2015a), 170–209.

Hahne, Ron and Ben Morea, eds. *Black Mask & Up Against the Wall Motherfucker: The Incomplete Works of Ron Hahne, Ben Morea, and the Black Mask Group* (PM Press, 2011).

Harvey, David. *Seventeen Contradictions and the End of Capitalism* (Oxford University Press, 2014).

Hillinger, Charles and Jack Jones. 'Residents Put Blame on Police for Uproar'. *Los Angeles Times*, 13 August 1965, 3.

History.com Editors. 'Watts Riot Begins'. *HISTORY*, 9 February 2010. www.history.com/this-day-in-history/watts-riot-begins.

Holloway, John. 'Afterword: Rage Against the Rule of Money'. In Federico Campagna and Emanuele Campiglio, eds., *What We Are Fighting For* (Pluto Press, 2012).

Johnson, Thomas. 'Race Relations: It May Be a Long Hot Summer'. *New York Times*, 30 April 1967, 193.

Khong, En Liang. 'The Moral Clarity of the Turner Prize 2018' (*Frieze*, 197, 2018). https://frieze.com/article/moral-clarity-turner-prize-2018.

Knabb, Ken, ed. *Situationist International Anthology* (Bureau of Public Secrets, 2006).

Knabb, Ken. 'The Situationists and the Occupation Movements: 1968/2011'. 2011. www.bopsecrets.org/recent/situationists-occupations.htm.

Kurczynski, Karen. 'Situationism'. *Oxford Art Online*. 2010. https://doi.org/10.1093/gao/9781884446054.article.T2086071.

Landsberg, Mitchell and Valerie Reitman. 'Watts Riots, 40 Years Later'. *Los Angeles Times*, 11 August 2005. www.latimes.com/local/la-me-watts-riots-40-years-later-20050811-htmlstory.html.

Lasn, Kalle. *Culture Jam: How to Reverse America's Suicidal Consumer Binge and Why We Must* (Quill, 2000).

Lasn, Kalle. 'The First Great Global Uprising'. 2010. www.adbusters.org/article/the-first-great-global-uprising/.

Lasn, Kalle, et al. *Meme Wars: The Creative Destruction of Neoclassical Economics: A Real World Economics Textbook* (Penguin, 2012).

Lewis, Paul. 'Tottenham Riots: A Peaceful Protest, Then Suddenly All Hell Broke Loose'. *The Guardian*, 7 August 2011. www.theguardian.com/uk/2011/aug/07/tottenham-riots-peaceful-protest.

Loewe, Sebastian. 'When Protest Becomes Art: The Contradictory Transformations of the Occupy Movement at Documenta 13 and Berlin Biennale 7' (*FIELD: A Journal of Socially Engaged Art Criticism*, 1, 2015), 185–203.

Luna Ray Films. 'Watts Riots'. *PBS – A Huey P Newton Story*, 2002. www.pbs.org/hueypnewton/times/times_watts.html.

Malik, Kenan. 'The Truth About "Cultural Appropriation"' (*ArtReview*, 69:9, 2017), 70–3.

Marcus, Simon, et al. *After the Riots: The Final Report of the Riots Communities and Victims Panel* (Riots Communities and Victims Panel, 2012). http://webarchive.nationalarchives.gov.uk/20121003195935/http://riotspanel.independent.gov.uk/wp-content/uploads/2012/03/Riots-Panel-Final-Report1.pdf.

Marks, Taylor. 'The Case for Civil Unrest: The Watts Riots and Institutional Racism'. 19 April 2017. http://blackpower.web.unc.edu/2017/04/the-case-for-civil-unrest-the-watts-riots-and-institutional-racism/, accessed 19 December 2018.

'Marquette Frye Dead; "Man Who Began Riot"'. *New York Times*, 25 December 1986. www.nytimes.com/1986/12/25/obituaries/marquette-frye-dead-man-who-began-riot.html.

The Martin Luther King, Jr. Research and Education Institute. 'Watts Rebellion (Los Angeles)'. https://kinginstitute.stanford.edu/encyclopedia/watts-rebellion-los-angeles.

McKee, Yates. 'Occupy and the End of Socially Engaged Art' (*E-flux*, 72, 2016). www.e-flux.com/journal/72/60504/occupy-and-the-end-of-socially-engaged-art/.

McKee, Yates. *Strike Art: Contemporary Art and the Post-Occupy Condition* (Verso, 2017).

McKillop, James. 'Mob Attempted to Cut Off Policeman's Head, Court Told'. *The Glasgow Herald*, 22 January 1987, 3.

McLaughlin, Malcolm. *The Long, Hot Summer of 1967: Urban Rebellion in America* (Palgrave Macmillan, 2014).

Moore, Tony. *The Killing of Constable Keith Blakelock: The Broadwater Farm Riot* (Waterside Press, 2015).

Morrell, Gareth, et al. 'The August Riots in England'. *National Centre for Social Research*, 2011. www.natcen.ac.uk/study/study-of-august-riots-in-england.

Murch, Donna. 'The Many Meanings of Watts: Black Power, Wattstax, and the Carceral State' (*Organization of American Historians Magazine of History*, 26:1, 2012), 37–40.

The National Advisory Commission on Civil Disorders. *The Kerner Report* (Princeton University Press, 2016).

'Negro Heroism Saves Whites in Riot Danger'. *Los Angeles Times*, 13 August 1965, 3.

Newman, Kenneth. 'Public-Police Relations: The Pace of Change'. *The Police Foundation Annual Lecture*, 1986. https://web.archive.org/web/20110721071915/www.police-foundation.org.uk/files/POLICE0001/speeches/1986%20Sir%20Kenneth%20Newman.pdf.

Nichols, Casey. 'Watts Rebellion (August 1965)'. In Sadie Plant, ed., *The Most Radical Gesture: The Situationist International in a Postmodern Age* (Routledge, 2002).

Rath Arun. 'Out of Long-Gone Rubble of the Watts Riots, Scars and Signs of Healing'. *NPR.org*, 8 August 2015. www.npr.org/2015/08/08/430753725/50-years-after-race-riots-watts-still-shows-signs-of-scars-and-healing.

Roediger, David. *Class, Race and Marxism* (Verso, 2017).

Roget, Stephan. 'Remembering the Watts Riots of 1965: Still Relevant as Ever (Sadly)'. www.ranker.com/list/watts-riots-facts/stephanroget.

Sadler, Simon. *The Situationist City* (MIT Press, 1998).

Schultz, Heath. 'Debord in Watts: Race and Class Antagonisms Under Spectacle' (*Lateral*, 7:1, 2018). http://csalateral.org/issue/7-1/debord-watts-race-class-antagonisms-schultz/.

Searle, Adrian. 'Turner Prize 2018 Review – No Painting or Sculpture, But the Best Lineup for Years'. *The Guardian*, 24 September 2018. www.theguardian.com/artanddesign/2018/sep/24/turner-prize-2018-review-tate-britain-naeem-mohaiemen-luke-willis-thompson-forensic-architecture-charlotte-prodger.

Sharlet, Jeff. 'Inside Occupy Wall Street: How a Bunch of Anarchists and Radicals with Nothing But Sleeping Bags Launched a Nationwide Movement'. *Rolling Stone*, 24 November 2011. www.rollingstone.com/politics/news/occupy-wall-street-welcome-to-the-occupation-20111110.

Shaw, Anny. 'Curators Defend Turner Prize Nominee Luke Willis Thompson'. *The Art Newspaper*, 4 October 2018. http://theartnewspaper.com/news/curators-defend-turner-prize-nominee.

Situationist International. 'Decline and Fall of the Spectacle-commodity Economy'. In Ken Knabb, ed./trans., *Situationist International Anthology* (Bureau of Public Secrets, 2006), 194–202.

Tate. 'The Politics of the Social in Contemporary Art – Conference at Tate Modern'. 2013. www.tate.org.uk/whats-on/tate-modern/conference/politics-social-contemporary-art.

Thompson, Nato, ed. *Living as Form: Socially Engaged Art From 1991–2011* (MIT Press, 2012).

Vaneigem, Raoul. *The Revolution of Everyday Life* (Rebel Press, 2001).

Viénet, René. *Enragés and Situationists in the Occupation Movement* (Autonomedia: Rebel Press, eBook version, 2014). www.cddc.vt.edu/sionline/si/enrages.html.

Wark, McKenzie. *The Beach Beneath the Street: The Everyday Life and Glorious Times of the Situationist International* (Verso, 2015).

Wark, McKenzie. *The Spectacle of Disintegration: Situationist Passages Out of the 20th Century* (Verso, 2013).

Weldon, Kathleen. 'The Long Hot Summer: Riots in 1967'. 2017. https://roper center.cornell.edu/long-hot-summer-riots/.

Wollen, Peter. 'The Situationist International' (*New Left Review*, I:174, 1989), 67–95.

2 Protest art and public space

Oleg Kulik and the strategies of Moscow Actionism

Marina Maximova

This chapter focuses on Moscow Actionism, the violent and spectacular strain of Russian performance art that emerged in the early 1990s in response to the collapse of the Soviet regime and transformation of life under the new capitalist order. The sudden and quite unexpected end of the Soviet Union resulted in fundamental and abrupt shifts in all spheres of social life. Arguably, one of the most dramatic transformations was in the understanding and functioning of the public sphere. In what follows, I argue that the emerging radical art practices of the 1990s, united under the umbrella term of Moscow Actionism, played a key role in redefining the parameters and conventions of public life and social behaviour.

The peculiarities of public space in Russia and the Soviet Union are defined by the specific and long-lasting experience of Soviet state socialism. This offers a striking contrast to the trajectories of the role and use of public spaces in Europe and North America. Even though the boundaries of the public/private dichotomy and the relevance of public space in the Soviet Union are still debated,[1] there is a considerable consensus among scholars that suggests that public spaces in the Soviet period were of limited use, due to extensive political control and surveillance, effectively turning the ideal of 'everyone's space' into 'no-one's space' (Zhelnina, 2013: 32). The emergence of new exclusive hierarchies from the 2000s onwards and developments in post-Soviet cities resulted in the loss of 'publicness'. (Darieva et al., 2011: 24). Hence, in contrast with preceding and following decades, it is notable that the public sphere occupied a particularly important and unique role in the 1990s.

In recent years, there has been an upsurge of scholarly and public attention on this particular decade. On the one hand, if compared to the 2000s, which are often described as 'a period of renovation and creation', the 1990s are traditionally portrayed as a 'time of destruction' (Henderson, 2011: 18). Boris Yeltsin, the new head of the state elected in 1991 in the course of chaotic events following the deposition of the last party secretary,

Mikhail Gorbachev, started the uncontrollable process of privatisation. The large chunks of previously publicly owned assets and resources were transferred into private hands. As the values and structures of Soviet life crumbled, organised crime emerged from the ruins (Galeotti, 2018). Violence, excess and greed came into fashion, affecting the ways that post-Soviet citizens went about their daily lives. Adjusting to the new reality changed the parameters of socially acceptable behaviour in sometimes shockingly unexpected ways (Esche, 2017: 49).

On the other hand, Russian liberal opposition often regards the 1990s as an era of growing civil freedoms, opening possibilities and self-realisation, which soon came to an end (Domrin, 2003: 195). In that moment of the State's retreat, its place was for a very short time taken by a civil society that was becoming increasingly active. Indeed, the end of the single-party rule and the restructuring of power, the democratisation of social institutions, the growing freedom of the press and changing attitudes towards dissidents combined with a hesitancy about conducting liberal economic reforms created truly unique conditions.

In what follows, I focus on Moscow Actionism as the most vivid manifestation of the changing approaches towards the public sphere. I will first discuss the emergence of the movement and the new understanding of 'location' that it introduced, specifically in relation to performance art. I will then turn to the practice of curator and artist Oleg Kulik, one of the central figures of this artistic movement, in order to further problematise the evolution of Moscow Actionism and identify its major stages.

The emergence of Moscow Actionism and the appropriation of public space

The roots of Moscow Actionism can be traced back to the action performed by the art activist group *dvizhenie E.T.I. (Ekspropriatsiia territorrii iskusstva)* [movement E.T.I. (Expropriation of the territory of art)] and titled *Vosklitsatel'nyi znak. (E.T.I.-tekst)* [Exclamation mark. (E.T.I.-text)] on 18 April 1991.[2] It was not the first action of the group, but, more significantly, it became the most talked about. Reviewing some of the debates that emerged around the work makes us better placed to decipher the context in which Moscow Actionism was initiated.

On 18 April 1991 a seemingly unremarkable group of young people arrived in Red Square. They walked to the vast open space in front of the Lenin Mausoleum and loitered around for some time looking anxious and perplexed. One of them, however, quickly took the initiative, ordering others what to do, and in no time the group was lying on the ground forming with their bodies the Russian word *ХУЙ* [*khui*, cock]. It took even less time for *militsia* [police] who looked equally puzzled and confused to approach the youngsters. When asked what they were doing, the initiator of the action, artist and activist Anatoly Osmolovsky, responded that they were 'making geometrical shapes with their bodies' (Osmolovsky, 2015: 45). He later repeated the explanation to the police officer in the station to which the youngsters were convoyed. Not knowing how to deal with or even how to define the accident, the officer recorded the names and addresses of all the participants and let them go (Osmolovsky, 2015: 45). The action was photographed by another participant, the correspondent of the major Moscow periodical *Moskovskii Komsomolets* [Moscow Komsomol Member], Anatoly Gusarov. He submitted the developed images to the newspaper, and the following day the picture and the short text reporting the event appeared in the press.[3]

One could argue that the *ETI*'s action was hardly more violent than the act of scribbling words on public bathrooms walls. It could also be seen as a naïve and childish performance, a manifestation of public mischief aimed at teasing the authorities and challenging the boundaries of accepted social behaviour. However, the action's significance lies in the fact that it highlighted the core feature of the new strategies of performance art that started to develop in the early 1990s and became key to the understanding of Moscow Actionism.

Three key features can be identified in the new performative strategies, exemplified by the kind of actions carried out by *ETI*. First, the location of the action was of crucial importance. This issue clearly manifested itself when members of the *ETI* group were accused of plagiarism by the participants of the conceptual art group *Mukhomor* [Toadstool].[4] The latter group, which by 1991 had already been broken up, became known in the early 1980s for their sarcastic performances and humorous objects (Obukhova, 2007). As one of its members pointed out, they had already done similar work and made the same word with their bodies on an empty snowy field several years prior to *ETI* (Zvezdochetov, quoted in Osmolovsky, 2015: 45). While the obvious similarities between two actions cannot be denied, the change of location from the deserted field to a crowded central square reflects the shift in the relations between the artists, space and the public, which occurred in the early 1990s.

During Soviet times, non-traditional and radical art practices, including performance art, were pushed to the margins of society. Moreover, it was often the conscious choice of artists to distance themselves from the public view.[5] Even when happening in central public locations, such as the Moscow underground or central streets, these practices were based on the inner discussion of the closed and exclusive Moscow conceptual circle and remained mostly unnoticed by the general public.[6] The kind of ambiguous position held by 'alternative' artforms in the late-Soviet years has been studied by a number of art historians and sociologists. Their work demonstrated that artists preferred to exist *vnye* [outside] (Yurchak, 2006) or to *drop-out* (Fürst, 2017) from the prescribed routine of Soviet life in order to find alternative spaces for their expression. The sphere of their existence was the 'shadowy' Soviet semi-private semi-public sphere, mostly based on personal networks and connection and significantly different from the public/ private dichotomy as understood more generally in the West. This situation came to an end with the fall of the Soviet regime and deconstruction of the norms that defined it. However, taking place a few months before the dissolution of the Union, *ETI*'s actions already reflected changing attitudes towards the use of space in art practice.

Responding to the allegations of copying, the ideologist of the group, Osmolovsky, claimed that the change of the location entailed a significant shift in the meaning of the work (Osmolovsky, 2015: 46). He argued that at the core of the *ETI*'s action was not the 'inscription of certain words with human bodies' but the realisation of the action on Red Square, probably Moscow's most ideologically loaded public space. As argued by another participant of the performance, Sasha Obukhova (then an art history student in Moscow Lomonosov University and currently the curator and archivist of Garage Museum of Contemporary Art, Moscow), the action was aimed at the 'de-sacralisation' of public space (Obukhova, 2012). Pertinently, Red Square was chosen as the place with the highest concentration of political power.

A second feature was that *ETI*'s practices were a direct reaction to the newly introduced Act on Morality of 1991, which prohibited the use of obscene language in public spaces. With a few rare exceptions, in the preceding decades alternative artists avoided direct commentary on current political affairs. *ETI* contravened this by staging an open artistic protest against the infringement of the freedom of self-expression. By taking their actions to central public spaces, artists manifested their intention to engage in public debate, which departed significantly from the tongue-in-cheek strategies of earlier artistic practices.

Lastly, *ETI*'s action also highlighted the importance of the public press for the development of performance art. As Osmolovsky later recalled, it was not the action itself but the photograph in *Moskovskii Komsomolets* that caused most public attention (Osmolovsky, 2015: 45). The reproduced picture was taken from such an angle that the word 'cock' was in a dangerous proximity with the word Lenin inscribed on the wall behind it, implying the two were equated. Notably, it was not the use of obscene language in public space but the use of it in relation to the 'father of the nation' that was most provocative.

While the press seemed to create the biggest controversy around the action, it also played an instrumental role in squaring the matters with the authorities. The beginning of the 1990s was the time of unprecedented power and influence of the 'Fourth Estate', which even the law-enforcement authorities could not ignore (Kovalev, 2007: 9). References to the event in the press implied a degree of legitimisation, transferring it from being viewed merely as simple hooliganism to being seen as an act worthy of public attention. The 'approval' of the mass media was particularly important at the time when such forms of actionist art were only starting to be developed, and there was no clear understanding of how it should be dealt with. In many cases, it was the press coverage that allowed the artists to escape serious punishment.

ETI's actions manifested a departure from previous forms of performance practice. They demonstrate a desire not only for artists to engage in the public sphere but also to generate a direct public response. However, the rapid and often uncontrollable development of social and political life in the 1990s soon made it evident that more radical artistic languages would be required to reach this goal. The following discussion of Oleg Kulik's practice will illustrate this development.

Oleg Kulik as a demonic exhibition-maker

Kulik arrived in Moscow from his hometown Kiev in 1986. In the next few years, Kulik gained recognition in the artistic community for his 'theory of transparency' and a series of Plexiglas sculptures developed with his partner Ludmila Bredikhina.[7] However, the collapse of the old structures, the attempts to replace them with new capitalist institutions and the buoyant, fierce and often brutal social and political life that accompanied all that forced him to review his practice. As a result, Kulik abandoned his studio space and focused on finding a way to be in more direct contact with the society he was trying to address (Kulik, 2017).

The first incarnation of Kulik was in 1991, when he became an *expozitsioner* [exhibition designer] at the private art gallery Regina.[8] This privately owned commercial gallery, established in September 1990, was run by Vladimir Ovcharenko, one of the many new Russian businessmen to emerge in the wave of perestroika. However, the principles of its functioning were very different from the traditional Western art gallery model (Diakonov, 2013). Regina was one of a host of galleries that were set up in Moscow following the end of the State monopoly on art sales. The new galleries were also inspired by the striking, if short-term, success of Russian art on the global market.[9] Ironically, what defined the scene at the time was total ignorance about how art sales functioned. Being funded by other non-art-related businesses of their owners, Moscow galleries of the early 1990s functioned as *Kunsthalle*, the forums for presentation and discussion of contemporary art. In the situation in which the old institutions had failed to readjust to the new order and new ones were yet to open, these commercial galleries operated rather like public art museums. Besides taking on the role of popularising and promoting contemporary art, they also developed new audiences for it.[10]

What precisely was Kulik's strategy in addressing and constructing new post-Soviet publics? To answer this question, one needs to consider the nature of audiences attracted by contemporary art. Throughout the Soviet years all types of artistic culture that challenged the confines of socialist realism had semi-permitted semi-public status, and, consequently, they were restricted to a relatively secluded existence. The limited audience for this kind of art was largely dependent on the circulation of information amongst the artists themselves, the liberal intelligentsia and educated youth. However, the growing openness of the country and the shifts in its social structures broke the previously closed and tight artistic community, forcing it to open up to new audiences and publics (Reid, 1989: 4).

This change was closely examined by curator and art theorist Viktor Misiano, who argued that in the 1990s a new type of community emerged. He called it *tusovka*, a Russian term for a gathering, a crowd, a 'coming-together' (Misiano, 2005). Unlike the exclusive model of the *circles of friends,* which was dominant in the previous decades, the defining feature of *tusovka* was its openness and democracy. There were no obstacles for joining, and the major criterion to enter such community was an ability to be in the right place at the right time. *Tusovka* was a type of a serial community, which only existed as a result of regular meetings. (Misiano, 2005). Kulik's practice as a curator became an attempt to facilitate the existence of this new type of community by creating discursive spaces for its gathering and 'coming-together'. The exhibitions that he produced in Regina should be understood less as static art displays and more as invitations for meetings and as a major vehicle for maintaining the existence of the new social structures. Thus, Kulik's early exhibitions became performances, where the traditional role of artists, artworks and viewers were challenged and subverted.

Soon however, Kulik shifted from the idea of creating exhibitions as a vehicle for producing new social structures to something much more critical. Exhibitions as social gatherings were quickly replaced by exhibitions as provocations. One of the first shows of this kind was *Apologiia Zastenchivosti, ili iskusstvo iz pervykh ruk* [Apologetics of shyness, or Art from the first hands], 27–28 June 1992. This exhibition consisted of a display of paintings from Ovcharenko's personal collection. Rather than being hung on the walls though, they were held by people hiding behind them.[11] Kulik's initial idea was that the works would be held by students or gallery friends (Kulik, 2017). He described this gesture as an attempt to add 'existential meaning' to what, otherwise, he saw as a display of works lacking any strong expressions (Kulik, 2017). Spending the event in a cramped space doing such uncomfortable work did not appeal to anyone, however. The problem was solved by Kulik bribing the commander of a troop of soldiers who were dispatched to the gallery for one night.[12] What was already a provocative exhibition technique thereby acquired new political connotations. The poor conditions of the army came as no surprise for many, but such an open act of corruption performed for the sake of the entertainment of the new creative elite seemed outrageous, even at that time.

The central role in this performance was taken up by Kulik himself. The footage of the event shows him arranging both the artworks and soldiers in the space.[13] Once the correct positions were taken, he continued managing the display, ordering the soldiers to hold their hands straighter and higher, arranging substitutions and making sure the works were in the right places. Kulik was followed by a troop sergeant double-checking all the arrangements. The presence of these two figures in the same space raised the issue of Kulik's power over the exhibition, allowing parallels to be drawn between the notion of authority within a military context and that within the context of an art space.

At the same time, the juxtaposition of the two figures can also be read as a commentary on the new social hierarchies and the emerging class of *novye rysskie* [new Russians], the small group of entrepreneurs who managed to benefit from privatisation to become the first Russian super rich.[14] This new social segment became the symbol of all the vices and pleasures of the perestroika period, characterised by the development of criminalisation and gang activities, dubious transactions through new private companies and, at the same time, excessive consumption and consumerist display. Representing one of the newly emergent enterprises of the new era, Kulik was keen to highlight his belonging to the new rich and powerful. He was driven around the capital in a Mercedes by a private chauffeur; he wore magenta jackets, the most notable element of *nouveau riche* style; he decorated himself with massive golden chains and watches. Was this a genuine attempt to emphasise belonging, or was it a sarcastic commentary on this new rich class within Russian society?

The opening night of *Apologiia* and Kulik's ambiguous role in it exposed the mechanisms of the new class system. The growing segregation of society was vividly illustrated by separating people in the gallery into two obvious groups. The footage of the opening reflects the atmosphere of confusion on both sides of the fake walls: on one side, soldiers spying on the invited visitors through the holes and on the other, viewers trying to discern whose hands were holding the paintings in front of them.

While such open bribing of the military would create a scandal in many parts of the world, this gesture remained relatively unnoticed among the wider social disarray in Russia. However, Kulik's next attempt to challenge the existing social structures took a much more radical form. The exhibition *Piatachiok razdaet podarki* [Piglet gives presents] opened on 11 April 1992 as part of the Festival of Installations *Animalisticheskie proiekty* [Animalistik projects], an event initiated by Kulik. The exhibition was nothing like a traditional art display. In fact, there was no art at all. The centrepiece of the event was slaughtering of a pig performed by a group of butchers invited by Kulik from a central Moscow market.

In this particular event, when unsuspecting visitors arrived at the gallery for the advertised *vernissage*, they found the venue split in half: one half was set aside for the audience, whilst the other was set out for the main action, the slaughtering of the pig. The installed TV allowed the crowd to nervously half-watch what was happening, while 'uncle Kolya came, put down a pig and forced a knife' (Ovcharenko, as quoted in Kabanova, 2011). The slaughter itself, however, was 'surprisingly short in time and not as spectacular as one would think' (Kovalev, 1992). The shocking and provocative action of slaughtering an animal was followed by the mundane activity of cutting the meat, which was then offered to the viewers upon the presentation of the gallery invitation.

Almost instantly, the event was surrounded by all kinds of rumours as reports of the inhuman *nouveau riche*, violently killing the innocent animal for their own entertainment, quickly spread across the city. The newspapers were full of articles with such titles as 'Let them pay for it!', 'Russophobia won't do!' or 'Pigs are eating humans'.[15] Some visitors and journalists pointed to the offensiveness of this gesture funded by the newly rich businessman and organised by the self-indulgent curator who gave charity to their poverty-struck audience by offering them free food (Barinov, 1992). Others claimed that the audience was no better than the owner of the space, describing them as bourgeois, high-heeled and well-groomed vampires, killers and sadists (Plotnikova, 1992). Animal rights activists gathered outside, trying to storm in and handing everyone flyers that read 'Make stupid experiments on yourself, not on animals' (Kovalev, 1992). Kulik created further controversy in a TV interview, when he claimed that the pig was called Russia and it 'embodied the country with its century-long complexes, which cannot be solved but can only be cut off' (Zaretskaya, 2003).

What was the purpose of staging this brutal performance in the art gallery? Since pigs are being slaughtered on markets every day, can it be seen as a violent action? As Kulik emphasised, it was not the fact of the slaughter of the pig per se that caused the outrage but the fact that such action was brought into the gallery space and became the centrepiece of an exhibition (Zretskaya, 2003). As described by the visitor at the event and a major researcher on Moscow Actionism, Andrei Kovalev, he experienced rather conflicting feelings when, together with many others, he received his slice of meat (Kovalev, 1992). On the one hand, he described his satisfaction with receiving a free slice of pork and his desire to get another maybe better piece, a reaction that can easily be understood given the shortage of good quality, fresh ingredients in Russian stores at that time. On the other hand, however, Kovalev reflects on the ethics of the whole event and, together with other observers, points to his resentment about the idea of 'devouring the cute, innocent and pretty Piglet, character of many fairy-tales' (Kovalev, 1992).

Kulik's curatorial gesture and the response to it acquired particular importance in the context of the uncontrollable process of privatisation. Previously publicly owned assets were carved up in the process, which was hardly less violent than the slaughtering of an animal. Gun crimes and racketeering were rapidly increasing as society was sinking into a maelstrom of almost unrestrained corruption, violence and criminality (Galeotti, 2018). By focusing on violence as the object on display, Kulik exposed and revealed society's structures and conventions.

This was Kulik's most controversial exhibition, but it was also his final show with the gallery as he left Regina in 1993. At that time the gallery was in the process of relocation to the new venue. In 1994, Regina occupied the ground floor of a bank office on a central Moscow street. The move marked a significant change in its strategy. The new venue was much more glamorous: all exhibitions now required special invitations, face-control met visitors at the doors, and the opening parties no longer welcomed experimental artists, but rather were often attended by high-rank politicians (Kulik, 2017). This change of the strategy together with a closure of a number of galleries in the early 1990s indicated the changing atmosphere of the Moscow art world. The enthusiasm and optimism of the early 1990s were vanishing. The emerging financial crisis meant that the new business class became hesitant about spending their money on radical art projects.

Kulik as a stray dog

After leaving Regina Kulik 'found himself on a street, without the means for existence and . . . running around like a stray dog' (Kulik, 2014). However, being 'discharged from the gallery duties' he acquired the chance to 'break into the ordinary everyday reality' (Kulik, 2014) and explore the potential of taking his practice to the streets. Despite the fact that the Regina gallery in the first years of its existence had been a publicly open and accessible institution, the events happening there were aimed at the limited art-going public. On the contrary, Kulik sought to explore the effect of his actions on wider unprepared audiences.

Regina's transformation was a very accurate representation of the changing social mood in the period. By 1994, the excitement and romanticised hopes for creating a new open and democratic country had slowly started to vanish (Ljubownikow et al., 2013: 158). The control and limitations of the communist state were gone, but the new reality of 'wild capitalism' did not lead to greater freedoms for everyone. The developing logic of consumerism subjected new codes of public behaviour, which threatened the freedom of artistic expression and artists' rights to operate in public spaces (Zhelnina, 2013: 35).

The escalating decline in the accessibility of public spaces and their potential to produce and support civic life led to new responses from radical artists. Following *ETI*'s action on the Red Square, Moscow Actionists continued their attempts to win back the right to use and be present in the public sphere. Violating the remaining bans of public behaviour, they adopted the strategy of 'public mischief', which took roots in Russian Futurism (Glisic, 2016: 200). The artists populated the most central culturally and socially important streets and squares. Artistic duo Vitaly Komar and Alexander Melamid organised a performance on Red Square where they tried to install a scrolling text at the front of the Lenin Mausoleum to cover the communist leader's name.[16] Anatoly Osmolovsky smoked a cigar sitting on the 10-metre central monument of Vladimir Mayakovsky, the famous Soviet poet.[17] The *Netsezeudik* group staged a performance that involved nailing two real human scalps in the middle of the same (Mayakovsky) square, just a short walk from the Kremlin walls.[18] Alexander Brener engaged in sexual intercourse in the middle of Pushkin square, another central location and a popular destination for Muscovite leisure time.[19] The attention paid by Moscow Actionists to populating the city turned the 1990s into the 'season of performances in social spaces' and the 'never ending outdoor art festival' (Kovalev, WAM: 9).

Kulik, however, once again resorted to galleries for support. In 1994, he started to collaborate with art dealer Marat Guelman, who opened a new gallery in November 1990. Guelman's gallery quickly acquired a reputation for its provocative, politically engaged shows. Guelman was not only not afraid to comment on the nation's most topical issues, such as the election process or the conversion of the Russian economy, but also encouraged the artists to do so (Degot and Tarkhanov, 1993). Guelman saw his ambition as an art dealer not so much to increase his profit and sales but rather to bring art into the centre of social and political life, provoking the audience for reaction and 'connecting the art to the energy of a bustling society' engaging new social segments and publics (Guelman, 1993).

On 23 November 1994, Marat Guelman knocked out the door of his gallery, located in the central part of Moscow. Barking and shrieking, Kulik jumped out onto the street. The artist was absolutely naked, running on all fours and behaving like a mad dog. With a horrible noise, Kulik attacked those invited by the gallery visitors along with random passers-by and jumped on the passing cars. As Vladimir Sorokin, a witness of the event, recalled,

> the face of the man in one of those cars was unforgettable. Imagine yourself driving home when a naked human-looking creature jumps on your front window spitting with furry. His facial expression made me think that he got the lesson of what the real Russia was with all its anarchic nature, savageness and unpredictability.
>
> (Sorokin, as quoted in Kravtsova, 2014)

Kulik's aggressive and behaviour can be seen as an experiment both to challenge the limits and possibilities of his own body as well as the minds and reactions of the spectators. In common with the slaughtering of the pig, this action can be read as a response to the conditions of the early post-Soviet society. However, being held in the atmosphere of the changing role of a public space, this action acquired different connotations highlighted in its title *Mad dog, or the last taboo guarded by a lonely Cerberus*. If Kulik was an embodiment of Cerberus, then what taboo was he guarding? Growling and biting in the middle of a busy central street, Kulik was defending the last remaining taboo in the public space that artists were allowed to break.

As Kulik recalls, the next day a number of Moscow periodicals came out with coverage of the event, which was depicted as the desperate reaction of an exhausted population forced to live like dogs (Kulik, 2014). Soon after that, Moscow mayor Yuri Luzhkov made a statement promising to 'clear the streets of the capital from naked and homeless people' (Efimov, 1994). The attitude of the city authorities towards managing the public spaces in the following years reflected this aspiration (Zhelnina, 2013: 35).

Kulik as a wild politician

In the mid-1990s, many of the problems of the Russian government and social order became even more apparent. Russian GDP fell by about 50% between 1991 and 1998, resulting in an economic crisis and market crash; the first Chechen war began in 1994; agricultural production reduced by 55%; life expectancy fell by five years (Nisnevich, 2013: 103). Inevitably, the nature of the artistic actions of the mid- and late-1990s reflected this changing social mood. Since the fight for the city was lost, many artistic projects were aimed at challenging the right of the authorities to represent society. The artists turned to developing and creating a whole range of alternative forms of politics.

One of the first direct artistic calls to the ruling power was the action of Aleksander Brener *Pervaia perchatka* [The first glove], performed on 1 February 1995. The artist appeared on Red Square wearing only a pair of boxer shorts. He stood on *Lobnoe mesto* ['forehead' place], a spot historically known as the place for monarchs to address their subjects. Putting on boxing gloves, he started to warm up in the manner of a professional boxer calling 'the coward Yeltsyn' to come and fight with him. In May 1998 an art group, *Vnepravitel'stvennaia komissiia* [Nongovernmental supervisory committee], organised an action, *Barrikada* [Barricade], which aimed to commemorate the anniversary of the 1968 protests. Two hundred and fifty activists blocked Bolshaya Nikitskaya street and built a barricade out of cardboard boxes just a stone's throw away from Red Square. Waving the slogans of French students, such as *Soyez realistes, demandez l'impossible*, the protesters prompted by the worsening economic conditions asked for life-long pensions and other clearly impossible social improvements from the government. In 1999, art group *Radek* organised an action during which its members climbed on top of the Lenin Mausoleum with a large banner which read *Protiv vsekh* [Against all]. The action was a sarcastic attempt to mobilise crowds before the upcoming Russian Duma elections.

The absurdist political strategies developed by the artists were, to their own surprise, applicable and effective in real politics (Kovalev, 2007: 12). Kulik offered his own vision of this, continuing the exploration of strategies for communication with mass audiences and using shock as his major technique. As with many other projects straddling the fields of art and political technology, the initiative came from Guelman. In June 1995, he launched an action-competition, *Partiia pod kliuch* [A ready-made party]. Guelman offered to cover all the expenses for establishing a party to a person whose political proposition would get the biggest number of votes. A number of artists and activists participated in the show, although rather than building an all-encompassing political campaign, most of the proposals focused on the individual desires, phobias and creative orientations of their creators (Kostiuchkova, 1995). As a result of the competition it was Kulik who won the funding for the establishment of his own party, titled *Partiia Zhivotnykh* [Party of animals].

Only a few days after the victory, Kulik started campaigning. First, he appeared on a central Moscow street wearing a muzzle and a chain around his neck and interrupted a dog show, whimpering and howling in front of the journalists. He later explained his action as follows:

> Today animals can't oppose the animal nature of humans. They are just puppets put on leads. I am fighting for animal's rights. I am their deputy in the elections.

> (Kulik, 1995)

In November of the same year, he notoriously claimed that 'being a homo sapiens is like being a fascist!' (Kulik, 2014) and used this slogan in his election campaign when he announced his decision to run for the presidency. His campaign poster included an image of himself passionately kissing a dog with the slogan: 'What problems can the greens have with us, little fellow?'

Kulik rarely communicated with his electorate using human language but rather mumbled as an animal. One of the most provocative meetings he organised was the action *Ne slovom, a telom* [Not with a word, but with a body][20] staged in April 1996 as part of the pre-election promotion aimed at collecting the signatures (Kulik, 2014). The process took the form of Kulik breastfeeding his supporters with vodka from teats attached to his stomach in two rows, mimicking the body of a mammal. This show attracted not only those who came to see the artistic performance but also those interested in what they perceived as a new party of nature-activists, in the process causing both indignation and confusion.

One of the most striking elements of the whole campaign is that, besides its obvious absurdity, it was still understood as a real political programme. The peak of Kulik's politic outreach was the discussion of his party in one of the major political TV shows *Namedni* [Lately]. As Kulik recalled, the party was presented not as an artistic provocation but as a realistic and witty way to steal at least 2–3% of the votes from Vladimir Zhirinovsky (a notorious far-right Russian nationalist) (Kulik, 2014). In the course of the discussion, the programme presenter, Leonid Parfenov, even claimed that the party could expect up to 30% of the votes (Kulik, 2014).

Describing his political experience, Kulik says that he was never interested in politics and always saw himself first and foremost as an artist (Kulik, 2017). Rather than a serious attempt to take power, for him this project was a way to expose the state of contemporary Russian political programme and strategy. In the 1990s, it was not a product of rational decision-making but a brutal drive to differentiate oneself, to take a stand. When Kulik finally brought his candidacy list to the electoral committee it was marked by cat's paws with flies and cockroaches glued to it. He was immediately kicked out, thus having to end his short political career.

Kulik as an international brand

Throughout the 1990s, many Russian artists tried to integrate themselves into the global art context with the aim of developing their practices in a marked attempt to distinguish themselves from any association with Soviet history. Kulik, on the contrary, became a recognisably Russian artist. He quickly realised, however, that, despite his work being a subversive response to the specific Russian conditions, it was very well-received in the West. Violence had a potential to be commercialised and exported.

The first re-staging of the *Mad dog* action took place in Zurich in 1995. Kulik, despite initially developing this work as a one-off performance, agreed to repeat it in Zurich Kunsthalle after being invited by curator Bice Curiger. Upon his arrival, however, he discovered that the invitation was a fake, a joke played by his fellow artists, so no one was expecting him to turn up (Kulik, 2017). Nevertheless, Kulik decided to make the most of the opportunity and organised the guerrilla action, re-locating it outside the museum. The naked artist chained himself to the entrance of the gallery, not letting anyone in, jumping at those who tried to pass by. Despite the atmosphere at first being playful and joyful, with visitors laughing at Kulik's foolery, the situation soon got out of control. When one of the impatient visitors stepped towards the entrance, Kulik emulated a guard-dog and dragged him to the ground. The action was terminated by the security of the Kunsthalle, and the police quickly arrived and arrested the artist.

The action revealed the important differences between the context and the position of an artist in a country with established rules of law and order in contrast with 1990s Russia, characterised by its transitional state of disorder and teetering legal order. Back in Russia, even when Kulik's actions were highly criticised, he was never detained. The special status that artists acquired at the time, their roles as showmen, media stars or simply 'urban crazy', protected them from legal consequences. The press facilitated such a situation. As Kulik (as quoted in Kovalev, 2007) recalled, at some point, journalists in Russia became so used to his role as a constant newsmaker that they were constantly asking him to keep them posted whenever he decided 'to do something crazy'. This was not the case in Zurich. Despite Western audiences being more familiar with radical artistic gestures and protests, the limitations were clearly demarcated by existing laws. Kulik violated the law as well as codes of behaviour in public places outside the exhibition space, and punishment was quick in coming.

However, this incident turned out to be rather favourable for Kulik. The next day, the Kunsthalle arranged bail, and the artist was released to find he was the subject of growing popularity. *Flash Art* even put Kulik's photo on their cover. As Kulik described:

> Strange things happened – my performance was presented as an extraordinary event and I started to be invited everywhere to perform a dog. Unexpectedly I was considered almost the major Russian artist.
>
> (Kulik, as quoted in Kravtsova, 2014)

This first re-staging of *Mad dog* was followed with what can be described as Kulik's 'world tour'. The following year, Kulik was invited by Viktor Misiano to participate in the *Interpol* exhibition in Stockholm, which focused on communication between Eastern and Western artists. Once again performing the dog, Kulik was given a designated space within the museum clearly marked by 'No Entry' signs, with a dog house in the middle of it. As in the first performance in Moscow, Kulik's reincarnation as a dog was shockingly realistic and extreme – the artist ran around as a mad guard-dog, keen to protect his territory. If any of the visitors walked too close or tried to contravene the signage, Kulik was ready to attack. Eventually when one of the viewers, who turned out to be a well-known Swiss critic, ignored the warnings, Kulik knocked him off his feet and bit him. Despite all the controversy, the action was repeated again in Rotterdam in 1996 where he was living as Pavlov's dog; the same year he appeared on Mariennplatz in Berlin, again in a dog's role protecting a European flag next to real police hounds. Later, in his dog persona he chained himself to a calf covered with a Union Jack in front of the European parliament in Strasbourg; finally he went to the United States in 1997, passing through the border control wearing a dog's collar and later exhibiting a performance, *I bite America, America bites me*, during which he stayed for a few days in a cage performing as a dog. This last action, which was undoubtedly a commentary on Beuys's infamous work, was not so much an attempt to fit Kulik's own practice into the context of global conceptual and protest art but rather a continuing attempt to exploit the image of a wild uncontrollable animal representing contemporary Russian reality.[21]

In 1997, Kulik also produced a series of staged photographs illustrating his potential family life with a huge black dog. Turning what had been a radical political public action into a number of tangible saleable art works, most of which were no longer provocative, this gesture marked the beginning of the end. By 1998, Kulik also started to be commissioned to 'perform as a dog' for special private occasions, such as parties in nightclubs or corporate celebrations. The format of a commissioned show for the sake of entertainment lacked the initial elements of unexpected guerrilla action and thus its initial political meaning. Kulik's transformation into an expensive brand was representative of the time when under the pressure of market institutions as well as increasing government control, civil society was dying out, giving way to the society of consumers (Mitenko, 2013).

Moscow Actionism emerged as a reaction to the misgivings of the Soviet art scene and as a response to disorderly and unpredictable political and cultural transition. Violence and provocation were adopted by the artists as the only appropriate response to the surrounding political and social conditions. The development of Kulik's practice and the transformation of his relations with society and the public sphere serves as a valuable example for attempting to understand the strategies of Moscow Actionism.

Kulik's actions and the use of violence, be it in the settings of the fashionable art gallery, on a busy Moscow street, at the pre-election campaign or in a famous Western institution, tested the limits of acceptability and thus exposed the inner mechanisms of the public sphere. The development of his strategies and actions illustrated the transformation of society and public space from the anarchic and uncontrollable to one characterised by increasing commercialisation and privatisation. At the same time, by turning violence into the object of display, he questioned its meaning in early post-Soviet society whilst also provoking viewers to question their own responses to it.

As the streets ceased to be the place for expression of radical opinions, artists were pushed from open public view back into the space of galleries and studios. Thus, actions aimed at the manipulation of social public space lost their initial meaning. Kulik's practice also changed considerably as he left his brutal projects behind. Instead, he explored new ways of impacting the audience, not through transgressive action or shock tactics but adopting more nuanced and often esoteric approaches.

Notes

1 The possibility of applying Western concepts of the public and the private to analyses of the Soviet Union has been criticised by several authors. The official ideology of the Soviets abolished any notion of the private property and saw the market as the root of all evil, and, thus, Western understanding of the split might not be relevant. Lewis Siegelbaum (2006) raises this concern in the collection of essays exploring 'private spheres of Soviet Russia'. Some scholars, such as Garcelon (1997), Zdravomyslova and Voronkov (2002) and Kharkhordin (1999), argue that instead of the traditional dichotomy, Russian society was characterised by the tripartite system. This third realm cut across public and private in the traditional Western understanding and was based on the networks of friends and acquaintances.

2 The group was founded by artist Anatoly Osmolovsky in 1989. Together with Osmolovsky its permanent members were Dmitry Pimenov and Grigory Gusarov. The participants of each of the actions varied. This action was performed by Grigory Gisarov, Aleksandra Obukhova, Milena Orlova and Anatoly Osmolovsky. The other participants were recruited just before the action, and their names are lost. The documentation of the action is held in the Archive of Museum of Contemporary Art Garage, Moscow.

3 The image and the short article title '*Vot eto vystupili!*' ['Look at them!'] appeared in the newspaper on 19 April 1991. The reproduction of the newspaper clip is available on Anatoly Osmolovsky's personal website, www.osmopolic.ru

4 The art group *Mukhomor* [Toadstool] existed between 1978 and 1984 and consisted of artists Sven Gunlakh, Konstantin Zvezdochetov, Aleksei Kamensky, Vladimir Mironenko and Sergei Mironenko.

5 An iconic examples of Soviet performative art practices was the Collective Actions group (Andrei Monastyrsky, Gerogy Kiesewalter, Nikolai Panitkov and Nikita Alekseev). Established in 1976, it became known for its performative actions, *journeys to the countryside*, which consisted in travelling to remote and deserted locations, such as fields and forests outside of Moscow, where some minimal, ritualistic and mysterious events took place. For more on the group see Monastyrskii, A. and Groys, B. (eds.) *Empty Zones: Andrei Monastyrskii and Collective Actions.* (London: Black Dog Publishing, 2011).

6 For example, on 28 October 1979, art group *Mukhoor* organised the action *Metro*, during which they spent the whole day in Moscow underground. Another example is an action by an art duo *SZ* (Vitaly Skersis and Vadi, Zakharov), for which throughout 1980 they covered Moscow streets with graffiti inscriptions *'Ai!', 'Oi!' 'Vot!'* [Here!]. In both cases it was important for artists to have their works embedded into the everyday Soviet life. At the same time their actions were created and discussed within the same closed artistic circle and, despite using the surrounding reality as their important element, rarely if ever provoked any response of general audience.

7 The theory defined the relations between art and surrounding reality. According to Kulik, art should not create anything new but should become a lens, which would expose certain elements of the reality. Kulik believes that he developed this idea in his following performance practice. His explanation of how he understands and uses the concept of transparency can be found in documentation of Oleg Kulik's workshop in the series *New Artistic Strategies* held in the Archive of Museum of Contemporary Art Garage, Moscow.

8 The term 'curator' was only starting to be used in Russian art context at that time. Throughout the Soviet period, the Russian word *kurator* was used to signify anyone entrusted with a supervision of something or someone. It had very strong negative connotations as it often referred to a KGB officer controlling the activities of the suspicious individuals. Kulik's position in Regina was titled *ekspozitsioner* [exhibition designer]. The function he exercised there, however, extended far beyond the design of the display and involved the development and often execution of the whole concept of an exhibition. In his retrospective assessment of his role during the interview with the author in 2017, Kulik insists that he was not a curator, as he 'did not add any new meanings to the works, but rather found the best ways to display them'.

9 On 7 July 1988 Sotheby's organised the auction of Soviet modern and contemporary art, during which many of the works reached record prices. It marked the time of the extreme increase of the demand for Soviet contemporary artists with many shows organised in both commercial and non-commercial foreign venues. For more information on the auction and its influence see, for example, Grisha Bruskin, *Past Tense Imperfect* (Moscoe: Novoe Literaturnoe Obozrenie, 2007), 301; Suzanne Muchnic, Soviet artists sceptical after historical auction, *Los Angeles Times*, 07 (1988); Simon de Pury, Russian art in the middle of attention, in Kate Fawle and Ruth Addison, eds. *Exhibit Russia: The New International Decade* (Moscow: Art Guide, 2016), 57–9; and Andrew Solomon, *The Irony Tower. Soviet Artists in a Time of Glasnost* (New York City: Knopf Publishing Group, 1991), 15–25.

10 Despite a number of attempts in the late 1980s to open the first Russian museum of contemporary art, the first collecting institution devoted to contemporary art, National Centre of Contemporary Art, was not opened until 1994.

11 It is important to note that the show had no commercial objectives since all works on display were from the private collection of Ovcharenko. This provenance of the works explains the diverse range of the artists included, starting from by that time already well-known ones, such as Kabakov, Orlov, Chuikov and Zvezdochetov, to the younger and lesser known names. The space of the gallery was significantly reduced by building the second set of walls, parallel to the existing structure, which left corridors between them.

12 It is still unclear if and how they were paid.

13 Documentary footage is available at www.youtube.com/watch?v=FjBjRYdJVzU

14 For more discussion of *New Russians* see Balzer, H., Routinization of the New Russians? *The Russian Review*, 62 (2007), pp. 15–36.

15 See Nagibin, Y., 'Svin'i poedaiut liudei. [Pigs Eat Humans]'. *Trud*, 15 April 1992; Barinov, D., 'Ubijtsy ot iskusstva [Murderers from Art]'. *Novy Vzgliad*, 25 April 1992; Plotnikova, M., Kotseptualisty muchaiut zverei [Conceptualists Torture Animals], *Kommersant*, 9 March 1992.

16 Action, '*Sueat suet*' [Vanity of vanities], April 1993, Red Square. Authors: Vitaly Komar and Aleksander Melamid.

17 Action, '*Mayakovsky – Osmolovsky*', 11 September 1993, Mayakovsky square. Author: Anatoly Osmolovsky.

18 Action, '*Gvozdi*' [Nails], 14 April 1994, Mayakovsky square. Authors: *Netseuzedik* group.

19 Action, '*Svidanie*' [Date], 19 March 1994, Pushkinskaya square. Author: Aleksander Brener.

20 The title was a play of words on the well-known Russian proverb *Ne slovom, a delom* [Actions speak louder than words].

21 Beuys's action *I Love America and America Loves Me* took place in May 1974 in a New York gallery, where he spent three days locked in a room with a live coyote.

Bibliography

Balzer, Harley. Routinization of the New Russians? *The Russian Review*, 62 (2007), pp. 15–36.

Barinov, Dmitry. Ubijtsy ot iskusstva [Murderers From Art]. *Novy vzgliad* [*New View*] (25 April 1992). Available at http://artprotest.org/cgi-bin/news.pl?id=3041 [accessed on 12 October 2018].

Bavil'sky, Dmitry. *Skotomizatsia. Razgovory s Olegom Kulikom* [*Scotomisation. Coversations with Oleg Kulik*] (Moscow: AdMarginem, 2004).

Darieva, Tsypylma, Kaschuba, Wolfgang, and Krebs, Melanie (eds.). *Urban Spaces After Socialism: Ethnographies of Public Places in Eurasian Cities* (Chicago: University of Chicago Press, 2011).

Degot, Ekaterina and Tarkhanov, Aleksei. Khudizkniki mogut polozhit'sia na Marata Gelmana [Artists Can Rely on Marat Guelman]. *Kommersant*, 199 (16 October 1993). Available at www.kommersant.ru/doc/62261 [accessed on 12 October 2018].

Diakonov, Valentin. 'Dlia vselennoi dvadtsat' let – malo': galerei 1990-h godov kak zakazchiki i populiarizatory iskusstva molodogo rossiiskogo kapitalizma ['20 Years for the Universe Is Nothing': Galleries of the 1990s as Commissioners and Popularisers of Art of Young Capitalism]. *ArtGuide* (18 September 2013). Available at http://artguide.com/posts/423-dlia-vsieliennoi-dvadtsat-liet-malo-ghalieriei-1990-kh-ghodov-kak-zakazchiki-i-populiarizatory-iskusstva-molodogho-rossiiskogho [accessed on 12 October 2018].

Domrin, Alexander N. Ten Years Later: Society, 'Civil Society,' and The Russian State. *The Russian Review*, 62 (2003), pp. 193–211.

Efimov, Sergei. Brodiag progoniat s ulitsy [Homeless Will Be Forced Out of the Streets]. *Komsomol'skaia Pravda* [*Komsomol Truth*], 65(5563) (1994).

Esche, Charles. Animal Magic: Oleg Kulik or How One Person Dealt With the Collapse of Everything. In Marat Gelman and Andrei Kovalev (eds.), *Art Riot: Post-Soviet Actionism* (London: ABCDesign Studio, 2017).

Fürst, Juliane. To Drop or Not to Drop. In Fürst, J. and McLellan, J. *Dropping Out of Socialism: The Creation of Alternative Spheres in the Soviet Bloc.* (Lanham: Lexington Books, 2017), pp. 1–20.

Galeotti, Marc. Gangster's Paradise: How Organised Crime Took Over Russia. *The Guardian* (23 March 2018). Available at www.theguardian.com/news/2018/mar/23/how-organised-crime-took-over-russia-vory-super-mafia [accessed on 12 October 2018].

Garcelon, Marc. The Shadow of the Leviathan: Public and Private in Communist and Post-communist Society. In J. Weintraub and K. Kumar (eds.), *Public and Private in Thought and Practice: Perspectives on a Grand Dichotomy* (Chicago: University of Chicago Press, 1997).

Glisic, Iva. From Futurism to Pussy Riot: Russia's Tradition of Aesthetic Disobedience. *History Australia*, 13(2) (2016), pp. 195–212.

Henderson, Sarah L. Civil Society in Russia. *Problems of Post-Communism*, 58(3) (2011), pp. 11–27. Available at www.guelman.ru/gallery/moscow/konvers/ [accessed on 12 October 2018].

Kabanova, Olga. Byvshii banker [Former Banker]. *ArtKhronika* [*ArtChronicle*] (16 May 2011). Available at http://artchronika.ru/gorod/бывший-банкир/ [accessed on 12 October 2018].

Kharkhordin, Oleg. *The Collective and the Individual in Russia: A Study of Practices* (Berkeley: University of California Press, 1999).

Kostiuchkova, Nina. Iskusstvo s narodom i bez nego [Art With People and Without Them]. *Segodnia* [*Today*], 120(478) (30 June 1995).

Kovalev, Andrei. *Rossiisky Aktsionism* [*Russian Actionism*] (Moscow: WAM, 2007).

Kovalev, Andrei. Zhertvoprinoshenie [Sacrifice]. *Ogoniok* [*Fire*] (24 April 1992). Available at http://artprotest.org/cgi-bin/news.pl?id=3035 [accessed on 12 October 2018].

Kravtsova, Maria. Kogda galieristy byli radikalami, a khudozhniki novymi russkimi [When Art Dealers Were Radical, and Artist Were Nouveau Riche]. *ArtGuide* (31 March 2014). Available at http://artguide.com/posts/559-koghda-ghalieristy-byli-radikalami-a-khudozhniki-novymi-russkimi [accessed on 12 October 2018].

Kravtsova, Maria. Sobakiada Olega Kulika [Dog Series of Oleg Kulik]. *Lenta* [*Feed*] (24 November 2014). Available at https://lenta.ru/articles/2014/11/24/kulik/

Kulik, Oleg. Interview with the Author (2017).

Kulik, Oleg. Moskvu posetila skul'ptura Dzheffa Kunsa [Moscow Was Visited by Jeff Koons's Sculpture]. *Kommersant* (9 September 1995). Available at [accessed on 12 October 2018].

Ljubownikow, Sergej, Crotty, Jo, and Rodgers, Peter W. The State and Civil Society in Post-Soviet Russia: The Development of a Russian-style Civil Society. *Progress in Development Studies*, 13(2) (2013), pp. 153–66.

Misiano, Victor. The Cultural Contradictions of Tusovka. *Khudozhestevenny Zhurnal* [*Art Magazine*], 1 (2005). Available at http://moscowartmagazine.com/issue/41/article/794 [accessed on 12 October 2018].

Mitenko, Pavel. Kak deistvovet' u vsekh na vidu [How to Act on the Public Gaze?]. *NLO*, 124 (2013).

Nagibin, Yuri. Svin'i poedaiut liudei [Pigs Eat Humans]. *Trud* [*Labour*] (15 April 1992). Available at http://artprotest.org/cgi-bin/news.pl?id=3397 [accessed on 12 October 2018].

Nisnevich, Yuri A. Postsovetskaia Rossiia: dvadtsat' let spustia [Post-Soviet Russia: Twenty Years Later]. *Polis. Politicheskie isledovaniia* [*Political Research*], 1 (2013). Available at https://lap.hse.ru/data/2013/04/21/1307881051/Полис%20Постсоветская%20Россия.pdf [accessed on 12 October 2018].

Obukhova, Aleksandra. Mukhomory [Toadstools]. *Khudozhestvenny zhurnal* [*Art Magazine*], 15 (2007). Available at http://moscowartmagazine.com/issue/47/article/938 [accessed on 12 October 2018].

Obukhova, Aleksandra. Predshestvenniki Pussy Riot [Predecessors of Pussy Riot]. *Kulturny dnevnik* [*Cultural Diary*]. Radio Svoboda (29 August 2012). Available at www.svoboda.org/a/24692291.html [accessed on 12 October 2018].

Osmolovsky, Anatoly. Khui na Krasnoi ploshchadi [Cock on Red Square]. In Svetlana Baskova (ed.), *Devianostye ot pervogo litsa* [*The Nineties From the First Hands*] (Moscow: BAZA, 2015).

Plotnikova, Maria. Kotseptualisty muchaiut zverei [Conceptualists torture animals], *Kommersant* (9 March 1992).

Reid, Susan E. From Artist Outsider to Absolute Bourgeois. *Art Monthly*, No. 131 (1989), pp. 3–7.

Siegelbaum, Lewis H. (ed.). *Borders of Socialism: Private Spheres of Soviet Russia* (Basingstoke: Palgrave Macmillan, 2006).

Yurchak, Alexei. *Everything Was Forever, Until It Was No More: The Last Soviet Generation* (Princeton: Princeton University Press, 2006).

Zaretskaya, Nina. Rossiiskoe sovremennoe iskusstvo v video formate [Russian contemporary art in video format]. Oleg Kulik. *TV Gallery* (26 March 2003). Available at: http://artprotest.org/cgi-bin/news.pl?id=3037 [accessed on 10 October 2018].

Zdravomyslova, Elena and Voronkov, Victor. The Informal Public in Soviet Society: Double Morality at Work. *Social Research*, 69(1) (2002), pp. 49–69.

Zhelnina, Anna. Learning to Use 'Public Space': Urban Space in Post-soviet St. Petersburg. *The Open Urban Studies Journal*, No. 6 (2013), pp. 30–7.

3   Project *sigma*

The temporality of activism

Vlad Morariu and Jaakko Karhunen

The following chapter will focus on *sigma*, a network of cultural practitioners that was active roughly between 1963–1965. This highly ambitious project involved a network of writers, artists, scientists and psychiatrists, including William Burroughs, Jeff Nuttall and R.D. Laing. Its successes were modest: the most tangible outcome of the project was the *sigma portfolio*, an expanding, self-published collection of texts (Trocchi, 1964), 'part manifesto, part manual' for art activism (Wark, 2011: 126). Its initiator and convener was Alexander Trocchi, the Scottish novelist, poet, Situationist and drug addict. Our intention is to present a close reading of *sigma* essays to explore the unfolding of an art activist logic within the programmatic texts of the *portfolio*.

The very legitimacy of the concept of art activism – or politically effective art – rests on a claim about the power and autonomy of art. This claim maintains that a certain political form is to be found in the very act of making art. Structurally similar to an Austinian performative (Austin, 1962; Searle, 1969; compare with Derrida, 1988), art activism is 'doing' politics with art.[1] It empowers communities and individuals and facilitates democratic access. Admittedly, one could differentiate among degrees of art's effectiveness. Boris Groys proposed that art becomes politically effective 'only when it is made beyond or outside the art market – in the context of direct political propaganda . . . its production, evaluation, and distribution do not follow the logic of the market' (Groys, 2008: 6).

We would like to observe how important the spatial metaphor is in Groys's claim. It is also common currency in the early history of artistic institutional critique. In this tradition, the question of the power of art is conceived in spatial terms: if the air in museums and galleries is unbreathable, then what one needs to do is to find new spaces outside, on the fringes of the system or at least inside autonomous zones within the system.[2] We would like to propose, however, that although spatiality is a necessary condition for the realisation of art's transformative power, it is not sufficient. The distinction

Groys proposes between (art) commodities produced, distributed and consumed on the art market and (artistic) political propaganda also stems from the purchase the latter have on temporality. Politically effective art articulates an ideological vision and imagination.

Whereas the market functions through the intervention of an 'invisible hand' – operating within the flattened time of commodity exchange – politically effective art has a purchase on how 'another world could be possible': an imagination for the future. Therefore, one needs to supplement the concern about spatiality with an equally important reflection on temporality. The question is not only where to 'do' politics with art but also when – hence the urgency of acting 'now' – and for how long – not merely bringing something into existence but considering its persistence, the point of time in which it is created and the kind of future it has.

Our aim here is to unpack the *sigma* other-logic, which in our view rests on a particular articulation of space and time. We are not glorifying *sigma* as radical practice; nevertheless, we believe that in *sigma*'s very concept, definition and creative (dis)organisation, there is a sense of visionary credence, and a powerful belief in the possibility of surpassing the status quo and resisting the apparent erasure of the future. *sigma* articulates, in our interpretation,[3] an interesting case for the power of art: but instead of a revolution, *sigma* proposed an insurrection; instead of confronting brute matter, *sigma* proposed a change 'in the minds' of humans; instead of representing politics, *sigma* attempted to 'do' politics through the anarchic production of an excess of writing and publishing. Can *sigma* be relevant in today's globalised world, precisely when, to put it in Mark Fisher's words, we experience 'the slow cancellation of the future' (Fisher, 2014: 2–29)?

The 1960s, violence and sickness

We will approach the context of *sigma*'s emergence obliquely, through a radiography of the early 1960s, proposed at the end of the decade by one of *sigma*'s main associates, Jeff Nuttall. A controversial personality himself, Jeff Nuttall's *Bomb Culture* is interesting precisely because it focuses on themes that are still actual: the shrinking of the imagination of the future; the widespread social malaise; and an acute sense of class and state violence.

Michael Horowitz described Nuttall's book as 'a primary source and manifesto for the post-Hiroshima generation' (Horowitz, 2004). Indeed, every corner of Nuttall's book is haunted by the vision of the world's demise, conjured by the potentiality of an irresponsible triggering of the atom bomb. 'Sick', the fourth chapter of *Bomb Culture*, begins with an acknowledgment of the decline of the Campaign for Nuclear Disarmament (CND) and of the anti-bomb movement, which Nuttall was a part of. At that date the gulf between what governments were saying and what governments were doing had become incommensurable. Moreover, it was increasingly difficult to speak to political power starting from shared frameworks of value. But this was not a failure of political power alone: society, as a whole, had lost its 'appetite for life'. It had become clear that

> society looked forward to the death it had contrived . . . that we our-
> selves even lacked the will of colonial dissidents, that none of us was
> sufficiently alarmed about extinction to force the murderers to put
> down their weapons, that society commanded nothing but contempt,
> much less dedicated labour or respect for law, that love, honour, faith,
> selflessness were as false in ourselves as in our elders, that the only
> effective thing to do was what we daren't do – riot and destroy the
> death machine in a demonstration of serious protest, that the only thing
> that we *could* do was sit in humiliation and wait for extinction.
>
> (Nuttall, 1968: 105)

The last two lines of this paragraph are particularly thought-provoking: they account for the slow substitution of the vision of what *had* to be done (the radical destruction of society in its current form of living) with a pragmatic-realist vision of what could be done: sit and wait for extinction. In a certain sense, if not entirely making the leap into post-ideology, this substitution already points to a shrinking of the space of ideological visuality. There is only one form of imagination possible – the nuclear mushroom looming on the surface of the earth, a replay of Hiroshima, in short, nuclear annihilation. Thus, the question is *not* what needs to be done but how to wait for the end.

Nuttall mentions three possible answers to this question: first, a depressive passivity and isolation; second, a hedonistic search for sensation and for the 'kick of the moment'; third, the loss of the ability to feel, the loss of affection for the fate of the other and a disaffected and nihilistic subli-mation into dark humour where all values are negated. Nuttall, as well as many of his collaborators – like Trocchi – embraced the latter, the 'humour of someone who was ill, sick' and whose publicly recognisable symptoms were used 'as a last banner to brandish under the noses of the squares as a syphilitic might display his chances to a puritan' (Nuttall, 1968: 107).

Bomb Culture resonates with diagnoses of contemporary culture, upon which we will return towards the end of this chapter. To anticipate, Nut-tall's insistence on illness – social illness but also self-induced corporeal illness (through the abuse of drugs) and mental illness – finds a corre-spondence in Franco 'Bifo' Berardi's and Mark Fisher's insistence on the anxious and depressed subjects of semio-capitalism (Berardi, 2009, 2011; Fisher, 2009, 2014). For Nuttall, sickness is as much real as it is symbolical of a range of much-celebrated counter-cultural practices. A telling example would be the writing that would become heroin addict William Burroughs' 'slaughterhouse carnival' of the *Naked Lunch* (Nuttall, 1968: 107).

It is, thus, understandable why Nuttall, along with a large part of the British counter-culture in the early 1960s, would feel drawn to R.D. Laing's attempts to politicise madness. Nuttall's 'Sick' cites at large from one of Laing's 'sigmatic' texts, a version of which had also been included in the *sigma portfolio*, before becoming the second chapter in Laing's *The Politics of Experience* (1967). Laing argued that mental illness was primarily a social and political concept. Equally preoccupied with the urgencies of the 'current time', the main point of his text is that psychotherapy fails unless it considers the individual within the nexus of his/her social relations (Laing, 1967: 39–48). Laing was critical of the psychotherapies that objectified the human being, thereby reproducing political violence. The result is 'a shambles. Bodies half dead; genitals dissociated from heart; heart severed from head; heads dissociated from genitals. Without inner unity, with just enough sense of continuity to clutch at identity . . . a half-crazed creature in a mad world' (Laing, 1967: 46).

The 'constant terror of inconceivable violence' (Nuttall, 1968: 127) is what had produced this sick, 'half-crazed creature in a mad world'. What is sickness, though? Elaborating from his *Divided Self* (Laing, 2010), Laing was already working on this question, and Nuttall followed: if values are to be rejected, then the distinction between the sane and the sick is untenable. From this perspective the antipsychiatric experiment in Kingsley Hall can be concieved as a case where sickness becomes an ideological form. The therapeutic community of Kingsley Hall was instizued in 1965 by Laing, David Cooper, Leon Redler and Joseph Berke – its guiding idea was that one needs to experience madness and take it to its ultimate consequences in order to emerge healed, at the other side.[4] As for Nuttall, sickness becomes the very ground on which a new culture is articulated:

> We were eaten up by repressed violence and we were soured by the constant terror of inconceivable violence being committed on ourselves and the rest of man [sic]. From this we had strugglingly produced a culture. . . . Sickness was, then, for many, a will to enact some definitive ceremony of violence that would spend the aggression inherent in the collective subconscious, exorcise it and thus leave society cleansed of fear, with a clear way out for our over-accumulated frustrated energies.
> (Nuttall, 1968: 132)

We would like to emphasise the 'ceremonial', i.e. symbolic, aspect of violence in Nuttall's thinking. Gillian Whiteley has written a seminal text that emphasises Nuttall's role as masterminder and promotor of happenings, performance and installation art, as well as his involvement in the clandestine counter-cultural press (Whiteley, 2011). The novelty of these cultural forms throughout the early 1960s can be comprehended as 'ceremonies of violence' – as the unrestrained multiplication of ephemeral artistic and cultural forms, merging spit, scat and blood with the violence of language, colonising the undergrounds of the cities. Much of this would characterise the vision of space and time unfolding in *sigma*, Alexander Trocchi's project, within which Nuttall was actively involved.

Originally from Glasgow, Trocchi edited the English literary journal *Merlin* in Paris in the beginning of the 1950s before moving to New York (Wark, 2011: 127). His best-known work is *Cain's Book* (1960), in which the author's alter ego, Necchi, tries to negotiate his way in the world via heroin abuse and by embracing his alienation from the bourgeois order. As McKenzie Wark notes, after the literary success of *Cain's Book*, the *sigma portfolio* made it possible for 'Trocchi to abandon literature and yet keep writing' (Wark, 2011: 129). Michael Gardiner suggests that Trocchi's political position formed while he was editing *Merlin* in Paris from 1952 to 1954 along coordinates similar to those we have just developed here: 'Faced with nuclear destruction and totalitarianism, a non-binaristic, non-"political" way of thinking politics had become necessary' (Gardiner, 2006: 79). What *sigma* interestingly adds is precisely the question of persistence through collective organisation: *sigma* was meant not only as spontaneous articulation of energies but also as sustainable cultural infrastructure.

The space-time of *sigma*

Sigma is a letter taken from the Greek alphabet and used in mathematics. The capital letter ($\sum$) is used to express the summation whereas the small case letter (σ) expresses standard deviation – the quantification of the difference between the mean value and each individual member of a group. Sigma, therefore, is a metonym: it maps symbolically the space of relational possibilities – the manner in which individual entities stand to each other or relate to each other in a group. For Alexander Trocchi, a prolific though inconsistent writer and one of the main characters of the 1960s counter-establishment, *sigma* was the abbreviation for the coming 'invisible insurrection' within which 'all men [sic] must eventually be included', whether they are aware of its existence or not. *sigma* would not designate an agenda or a political group. In the foundational manifestos there is no trace of identification with traditional political polarities of left and right: it refuses traditional party politics and all kind of patronisation of art and culture by political vectors. The term *sigma* was to be used rather in its adjectival sense (i.e. *sigmatic*), pointing to a range of creative practices, programmatically laid out by Trocchi in two founding texts: *sigma: A Tactical Blueprint* and *Invisible Insurrection of a Million Minds*. These essays articulate the kernel of what became the main tool for *sigma*'s activity – the publication and distribution of the *sigma portfolio*, a collection of texts meant to reach their destinations through the mail but also by other means of clandestine distribution.

The programmatic texts of *sigma* are concerned with the analysis of 'the current situation'; both in the sense of 'present time' (in relation to the impossibility of a future emerging from the conditions of possibility of the present) and in relation to space, geography and political economy. From this point of view, Trocchi observes that the modern world has the capacity and the resources to solve the problem of production. As he explains, '[T]he urgent problem of the future is that of distribution which is presently (dis)ordered in terms of the economic system prevailing in this or that area' (INV: 2).

In 1963, when this text was first published, Trocchi's main concern was not production or the necessity of labour or work time spent within the process of production, such as it was discussed in classical Marxism. Nor was it the problem of distribution. Trocchi argued that the problem of wealth distribution is principally an 'administrative one' and that it can potentially be solved on a global scale by institutions such as the United Nations (INV: 2). In other words, the system has the capacity to take care of itself and regulate any dysfunctionalities in production and distribution. One way or another, Trocchi thought that distribution would eventually be solved through a better organisation of the institutional nexus. Turning his attention from these topics, Trocchi used the *Invisible Insurrection* to examine the perceived loss of leisure and leisure time. In other words, Trocchi argued that his contemporaries were incapable of giving themselves free time.

We will approach the distinction between the structures of work time and leisure time later; at the moment it should be emphasised that this distinction rests on a particular conception of one's situatedness in time and space. Trocchi proposed that few people realised that an evolutionary change had taken place: an evolution that had occurred 'in the minds of men [sic]' triggered by an awareness 'of the implications of self-consciousness' (BLU: 1). This change first took place in modern science, with the change of perception of what 'an objective world' meant: that the perception of the world is not and cannot be objective, that it is implicated in the way that the world appears. Likewise, a change had taken place in what came to be known as modern art, with its 'destruction of the conventional object'. In fact, Trocchi conceived art as capable of expressing this evolutionary change, while science offered the means through which one could hope to identify and solve the problems of situating oneself in this new historical age.

Having a first-hand experience of a range of new cultural and artistic ceremonials (happenings, installations, objectless art), Trocchi came very close to defining a new understanding for contemporaneity of life. And this took place well before the advent of conceptual art as well as before the emergence of 'contemporary art' in Peter Osborne's sense of post conceptual art (Osborne, 2013). Contemporaneity is the coming together of disjunct subjective temporalities, disciplines and practices, which call for the destruction and re-composition of life, thought and sensibility. The sudden conjunction of these elements calls for a new mode of expression. Hence the necessity of reconfiguring the 'grids of expression', the need to find new concepts, at the level of the language in general but also at the level of specific languages: the language of literature, for example, with the destruction of traditional canons or the language of art, which cannot be but reconfiguration of the traditionally separated arts or, the language of space, the conceptual matrix through which space is appropriated but also the sciences of space – architecture and urbanism. For the activities of *sigma*, as Trocchi suggested numerous times, can and must take place under the auspices of newly designed and newly created urban spaces.

The change should be conceived at the level of concepts, frames of thought and language: it has to do with the power of thought, with imagination and creation. Such a change would be attainable if representatives from all of areas of knowledge production were brought together in a common enterprise:

> We are writers, painters, sculptors, musicians, dancers, physicists, biochemists, philosophers, neurologists, engineers, and whatnots, of every race and nationality. The catalogue of such a reservoir of talent, intelligence, and power, is of itself a spur to our imagination.
>
> (BLU: 3)

According to Trocchi, this insurrectionary 'awakening' is not accessible to everybody. Much of the incapacity to come to one's own conscience of contemporaneity is caused by a lost sense of freedom in relation to time: the inability to understand how to use our free time. The majority of humankind had forgotten how to fill leisure time because lives had become mechanised and technologised. Trocchi's predicament is not far removed from our experience of everyday life in the digital age where, to put it in Berardi's terms, not only the body but the soul, too, is at work (Berardi, 2009). The mechanisation and technicisation of human lives are mirrored in the fact that free time is spent in the mechanical flux of news – today augmented by the semiotic fluxes of capital (from advertising to social media) – and where everything presented as 'new' is, in fact, a zombified repetition of the same. Vision, visuality and imagination in the contemporary condition are codified by the logic of the return of the same.

As an insurrection occurring in time and place, Trocchi believed that *sigma* could only insert itself into the capillaries of repeated uncreative time, in the undergrounds of the urban centres and in such a way that it would change time and space from within. This is the reason why *sigma* could not be a revolutionary, momentous change in time-space – an event that dies immediately as it comes into existence. This is also why it could not occur democratically as a movement of forces through existing space-time: the democratic choice does not exist yet because it cannot be imagined and visualised yet. *sigma* is not a *coup d'etat*, in the manner in which Lenin and Trotsky understood it. It is rather a *coup de monde*, 'more gradual, less spectacular' – an eminently cultural virology, which begins by intelligence becoming self-conscious.

Trocchi appears to believe in a kind of dialectic of historical violence, where 'revolution follows repression and is followed by repression' (GEN: 2). Thus instead of arguing for a revolutionary *coup d'etat* that would be swiftly and violently repressed, Trocchi envisioned an invisible insurrection fuelled by 'the powerhouse of the mind' (INV: 1). The enemy, writes Trocchi, is never personal: the real enemy is 'spiritual ignorance breeding fear, hysteria, schizophrenia' (GEN: 2). As the state is ultimately comprised of individuals, it is simply ignorance against what one must operate upon. Even war and violence exerted by the state appears to originate in thought. Therefore, the change in the consciousness of individuals is all that is required for a *sigmatic* rupture of the world.[5] 'What must occur . . . is a revelation', which includes the perception of 'the forces that are at work in the world';

> then, calmly, without indignation, by a kind of mental ju-jitsu that is ours by virtue of intelligence, of modifying, correcting, polluting, deflecting, corrupting, eroding, outflanking . . . inspiring what we might call the invisible insurrection.
>
> (INV: 2)

The metaphor of the 'mental ju-jitsu' here is borrowed from the Japanese martial arts: it is the art of defeating an armed opponent without the use of a weapon. It suggests hard work, self-discipline and a vigorous mind taking hold of itself, understanding its relation to the forces influencing the world – but also performing a creative and imaginative leap of faith that seems to be based on nothing but itself. A mental ju-jitsu is not a figure of aggression, though it is a figure of combat. It suggests the idea of a *sigmatic* insurrection taking place without aggressive weapons and only through the superiority of mental discipline. And, just like in the case of ju-jitsu, the awakening of these mental forces is available to everybody. The trick here is to *give oneself time*: the time freed by the gesture of rupturing fluxes of (fake) news or the time to see oneself as part of the nexus of social relations or even the time of a spiritual voyage, which may or may not be induced by drugs. *sigma* is precisely the opening of time when time only promises to come to an end.

Radical pedagogies

We claimed that the *sigmatic* insurrection should be understood in terms very much different from a Leninist doctrine of state conquest. This can be seen from *sigma*'s emphasis on spontaneity, which Lenin had already critiqued more than half a century earlier. Lenin suggested that 'the "spontaneous element" [in the workers' movement], in essence, represents nothing more nor less than consciousness in an embryonic form. Even the primitive revolts expressed the awakening of consciousness to a certain extent' (Lenin, 1999: 17). Yet, for Lenin, embryonic consciousness is able only to cater to the immediate interests of the working class and is useless for its complex organisation. Only conscious mediation and reflection upon its own conditions of existence in the social totality would make it possible for the working class to realise its revolutionary potential.

How, then, does *sigmatic* spontaneity support the task of seizing the 'grids of expression'? What facilitates the spreading of the *sigmatic* mental ju-jitsu? One concrete suggestion was the establishment of a 'spontaneous university'. At least in principle *sigma* rejected central coordination and organisation; indeed, if anything, the spontaneous university – the instituted gathering of artists, scientists, architects, urbanists, musicians, dancers, neurologists and philosophers – was theorised as *non-hierarchical, non-structural and non-organisational*. The spontaneous university retains the idea of 'universality' but rejects the specialisation of disciplines and 'disciplined technicians' and experts of knowledge – the outcomes of the nineteenth-century Humboldtian university project.

There is no room in the spontaneous university for examination-based curriculums, precisely because they encourage competition and the exhibition of 'virtuosity' in particular areas of knowledge production. Instead, the new university would gather an international network of imaginative teachers and students, housed in a large country house, not too far from London (and, later, other metropoles), placed (necessarily) on a river bank. The traditional boundaries between teachers and students would be eliminated: what is essential here is 'a new conscious sense of community-as-art-of-living' where 'the experimental situation (laboratory) with its personnel is itself to be regarded as an artefact, a continuous making, a creative process, a community enacting itself in its individual members' (BLU: 5). The pilot project was to be started in England, but Trocchi envisaged an international network of such universities to where its cosmopolitan members could travel, reside and engage with the local community.

The revolutionary potential of the million 'liberated' minds is based precisely on the unleashing of creativity, imagination, vision and visuality, freed from the automatisms of colonised leisure time, freed from the hierarchical structures of an institution. It is rather what exits, deserts and abandons, both spatially and temporally, the traditional environments for education, seen as conventional, violently reinforcing the status quo and feeding off state bureaucracies. Indeed, if there is a model for the spontaneous university, it is a model of flight, secession and desertion: as Trocchi suggests, just as Oxford broke away from the Sorbonne and Cambridge broke away from Oxford, the spontaneous university should break away from the existing educational paradigms, for only this flight would create the conditions for intelligence and creativity to emerge: 'Secession by vital minds everywhere is the only answer' (BLU: 4).

Integral to the *sigma* project, we argued earlier, is an attempted rearticulation of contemporaneity, as a conjunction of practices, disciplines, temporalities and spaces. It is not surprising, then, that a particular emphasis is placed on architecture and urbanism. Both *sigma: A Tactical Blueprint* and the *Invisible Insurrection* emphasise the roles that architects would take. They were to redesign not only spaces for creative sharing, education and knowledge production but entire miniature towns where *sigma* members could live and work. Ideally, these centres would be located close to metropoles – they would have access to cultural phenomena happening in the bigger settlements. Trocchi calls this process 'in(ex) filtration'. It is essential that these 'astronauts of inner space' would situate themselves amid new architectural settings because 'integral art cannot be accomplished except on the level of urbanism' (INV: 5–6). Changes in architectural space directly trigger changes in sensibility, thought and conceptual patterns. The concrete models offered are quite interesting: Eton College (a place of excellence unable to keep pace with time and becoming conservative), Jewish settlements in Israel and the much celebrated Black Mountain college (Miller, 2018; Molesworth, 2015; Katz et al., 2013).

The idea, therefore, is not to escape or go into exile as a total abandonment of the spaces and temporality one flees from:[6] infiltration in the urban matrix, where life follows the rhythms of capitalist work-time, is necessarily supplemented by exfiltration in the ecology of the spontaneous university, a veritable 'experimental laboratory', giving birth to a

> community-as-art [which begins] exploring the possible functions of a society in which leisure is a dominant fact, and universal community, in which the conventional assumptions about reality and the constraints which they imply are no longer operative, in which art and life are no longer divided.
>
> (BLU: 5)

Infiltration feeds from exfiltration inasmuch as the spontaneous university needs the capitalist economy of production, distribution and consumption to become economically sustainable. For Trocchi, the university needs to be an 'autonomous, unpolitical, economically independent' (INS: 7) enterprise. It would function, for example, as an agency for recruiting young talents. Its profits would be reinvested in spreading the net and making the message more widely available, while those signed on would be granted immediate membership.

Moreover, a limited liability company would be devised (tentatively called *International Cultural Enterprises (Ltd)*), whose profits were to be invested in the research and expansion of *sigma*. Its income would derive from selling original artworks; from 'patents'; from retail; from Situationist, theatrical or cinematic shows and other cultural activities. Finally, income could also be generated by 'cultural consultancy', as *sigma* members could offer consultancy services to buyers 'against the depreciation in value of any work or art recommended by *sigma*' (INV: 7). What we are reading here is a pragmatic approach to organisation that has already abandoned the pleasures of utopian imaginary;[7] the *sigma* insurrection embraces the capitalist economy to dismantle it from within.

Seizing the 'grids of expression'

The 'spontaneous university' is one of the means through which the grids of expression are seized, and indeed, one of the main roles of the spontaneous university is to rework inherited means of communication and expression, through the creative intersection of various areas of knowledge production. Language takes a central part in Trocchi's programmatic texts, since they acknowledge that the transformations in science and art made obvious another fact: that the nature of all languages is relative. And if language is relative, then the question what and how to learn needs to be reconsidered:

> Most of our basic educational techniques have been inherited from a past in which almost all men were ignorant of the limitations inherent

in any language. They will be men and women who are alive to the fact that a child's first six years of schooling are still dedicated to providing him with the emotional furniture imposed on his father before him, and that from the beginning he is trained to respond in terms of a neuro-linguistic system.

(BLU: 5)

We would like to note here that the conceptual reconfiguration emphasised by *sigma*, within the 'spontaneous university', presupposes a process of 'unlearning' or 'de-schooling',[8] as a prerequisite to a recodification of language and of the communicative situation and its instances. It would be the concepts of art and literature and their specific languages that have to be occupied, in order for such a conception of unlearning to be possible.

Here is where one finds Trocchi's other-logic, which faces a certain conceptual poverty: the way in which Trocchi uses the concepts of art and literature are subtly different from the type of art and literature produced, distributed and consumed on the capitalist market of the 1960s. Trocchi does not promote the obstruction of the production of art literature as exchange commodities. There is no problem with artistic production in the sense that artistic and literary products emerge at all times, under different socio-economic conditions, including capitalism. The situation is analogous to the actual production of goods, which should not pose a problem for the highly technical stage of capitalist production, while distribution can potentially be solved with better management. Thus (and we paraphrase Groys, 2008: 6 here), we could say that there is no problem with the fact that at least a part of the production of art is easily incorporated in the capitalist distribution flows and consumed as exchange commodities. The problem, once more, is when such a system prevails – when the ideological horizon of other types of production, distribution and consumption of art and literature is shut off.

For Trocchi, there is little in the 'official' art or literature of the 1960s that was able to 'awaken' and 'shake' consciousness. And by that he means works that can bring about '[the] situation in which life is continually renewed by art, a situation imaginatively and passionately constructed to inspire each individual to respond creatively, to bring to whatever act a creative comportment' (INV: 3).

In other words: literature and art are produced, but they are deemed weak and ineffective – and effectiveness is to be understood here in a political sense. Politically effective art and literature are necessarily insurrectionary. Interestingly, the model that Trocchi follows is jazz, precisely because of its history – it being an artform born from the experience of/consciousness of oppression and precisely because it 'retains the spontaneity and vitality deriving from its proximity to its beginnings' (INV: 3–4). Jazz is the artform that manages to bridge the gap between life and art and not Dada, as conventional wisdom claims. Indeed, Trocchi saw Dada as useless precisely because of its incapacity to produce an 'alternative to the existing social order. What were we to do after we had painted a moustache on the Mona Lisa?' (INV: 4).

For *sigma*, then, one of the most stringent problems was to creatively invent new means of distribution for art and literature that would interrupt the mechanised flux of news colonising our free time. Pamphlets and pamphleteering, for example, are seen as pivotal, just as much as any other expressive tactics that would break through traditional media: advertising in the space of little magazines, the personal columns of national newspapers, labels, matchboxes, toilet paper, cigarette cards, the back of playing cards, etc., as much as writing entire books. In the *Invisible Insurrection* Trocchi imagined 'a publishing project' that would occupy the advertisement panels of London Underground stations for one year and where a monthly or weekly magazine would be printed. 'And why stop at London? (Undergrounds of the World Unite!)' (BLU: 2).

This project was, in fact, put into practice and resulted in the *Moving Times* poster: a large A0-size off-set print with literary texts signed by, among others, Trocchi and William Burroughs. The poster itself was unspectacularly devised: various texts of different lengths were placed in rectangular boxes, separated from one from another. The texts were conventionally signed by their authors. But it is evident that both the formal layout, based on vertical and horizontal lines and the content of the assorted texts, are expressions of the same idea – of creative disunity, textual and visual articulation without any central theme or core. *Moving Times* – the times in movement, the temporality that moves from a standstill – seem to capture the times when such literary productions, published and shown under these conditions of production and distribution, are happening. The texts themselves present a mixture of 'fragments' of literary pieces, paragraphs from manifestos and allusions to the *sigma portfolio*. Not many issues of the *Moving Times* have been published, and the poster itself looked, indeed, quite unfamiliar to the potential reader (Trocchi and Nuttall, 1965). Closely following Brecht's *Verfremdungseffekt*, Trocchi did, indeed, suggest that one of the objectives of *sigma*'s production and distribution is to break down the dichotomy between creator and spectator, using the unfamiliar as a tool.

Sigma and the contemporary

In 'Sick', the fourth chapter of his *Bomb Culture*, Nuttall recalled that 'Alex Trocchi once told me he first took heroin for the sense of inviolability it

gave him'. And then he continued: 'If the cool hipster is severed from iden-
tificatory processes and thus from other people's pleasure and pain, he is
nevertheless an athlete of time' (1968: 133). Drugs have surely been one
of the counter-culture's preferred means to buy time for unlearning what
has been learned and for exploring the 'astronautics of the inner space'.
For Nuttall, drugs, together with an excessive emphasis on movement and
mobility, celebrated in the 'mobile arts, poetry, jazz, theatre, dance and
clothes' of the early 1960s, had already proven to be 'good tactics but a poor
alternative to the established culture. [They are] the temporary denial of
existence and existence must be our ultimate province' (1968: 243). *Bomb
Culture*, published during the period of the 1968 student riots and occupations would, in fact, claim that:

> [I]t is now necessary to come back from inner space. Having revived
> the faculty of wonderment it is necessary to apply it. . . . If we cannot
> translate the spiritual into terms of constructive physical action, if spiri-
> tual vision cannot inform our physical ocular vision, then the spiritual
> is none of our damn business.
>
> (Nuttall, 1968: 242)

Nuttall's predicament seems to apply directly to Trocchi, one of the 1960s
'athletes of time' and an 'astronaut of the inner space'. One cannot fail to
observe the inner contradiction between Trocchi's lifelong addiction and
the sense of inviolability in the claims of *sigma*. The invisible insurrection
was supposed to be inevitable and already underway: 'It is happening all
over the world' (GEN: 3). There is much 'tentative optimism' here, based
on the reading of myriad 'happenings': 'Joan Littlewood's experiments,
and Burroughs', Laing's post-Sartrean psychotherapeutic techniques, or the
Meat Science Essays of M. McClure' (GEN: 4). It is a legitimate question in
relation to *sigma*, whether this optimism was at all warranted.

From the perspective of a certain kind of realism – the realism of 1960s
capitalism, but also, more importantly, from the perspective of the realism
of our capitalism – optimism emerges against all odds, against the reality of corporeal and mental illness and against the seeming impossibility
to imagine a future other than the future of atomic extinction or planetary
catastrophe. We have suggested that *sigma*'s diagnoses of the 1960s bear
resemblance to our contemporaneity and it is here, towards the end of this
chapter, that we would like to develop this thought. Is there something in
sigma that remains relevant for the ways in which we think about art's
autonomy and art's power to 'do' politics? To ask about the warranty of
political optimism, precisely in relation to art politics and art activism, is to
ask: why hope? and why resist?

We would like to approach these questions through a brief consideration of two authors already mentioned in this chapter: Franco 'Bifo' Berardi and Mark Fisher. What is of interest to us is the manner in which they have considered the relation between our contemporaneity and the imagination, vision, visuality and ideology of possible futures. Berardi identifies an unyielding trust in the future in the historical avant-gardes of the first seven decades of the twentieth century, fuelled by utopian imagination and ideology of progressive future. In the aftermath of 1968, however, utopia transformed into dystopia, and the last utopia of the twentieth century – the cyberculture that wired the brain to cyberspace and cyber time – ended in mental exhaustion. What seems to characterise our current semio-capitalist, post-cyberculture condition is depression – economic depression but also corporeal fatigue and mental depression. He writes:

> The future becomes a threat when the collective imagination becomes incapable of seeing alternatives to trends leading to devastation, increased poverty and violence. This is precisely our current situation, because capitalism has become a system of techno-economic automatisms that politics cannot evade. The paralysis of the will (the impossibility of politics) is the historical context of today's depression epidemic.
>
> (Berardi, 2011: 59)

Berardi's 'paralysis of the will' points to a real foreclosure of the horizon of any future politics, and his thought finds an echo in Mark Fisher's *Ghosts of My Life* (2014), whose first chapter glosses over 'the slow cancellation of the future': the disappearance of the future, most visible in the realm of contemporary culture, where time, instead of going forwards, runs backwards, in a constant return of zombified revivals of cultural forms and styles:

> If the late 1970s and early 80s were the moment when the current crisis of cultural temporality could first be felt, it was only during the first decade of the twenty-first century that what Simon Reynolds calls 'dyschromia' has become endemic. This dyschromia, this temporal disjuncture, ought to feel uncanny, yet the predominance of what Reynolds calls 'retromania' means that it has lost any *unheimlich* charge: anachronism is now taken for granted.
>
> (Fisher, 2014: 14)

Both Berardi and Fisher are amongst the strongest advocates for a repoliticisation of mental health, following the attempts of Foucault, Laing, or Deleuze and Guattari in the 1960s and 1970s. Both argue for a direct link between semio-capitalism or – 'capitalist realism' (Fisher) – and depression. Fisher describes the realism of capitalism as a 'deflationary perspective of a depressive who believes that any positive state, any hope, is a dangerous illusion' (Fisher, 2009: 5), whilst the first chapter of his *Capitalist Realism* claims that it has become easier to image the end of the world than the end of capitalism.

For Fisher, himself battling depression, there seems to be little hope for a strategy of de-cancelling future. However, Berardi struggles to find an answer to the question: where is the hope? His answer is bafflingly simple: we must resist because we simply do not know and cannot know what will happen after the future, 'and I must preserve the consciousness and sensibility of social solidarity, of human empathy, of gratuitous activity – of freedom, equality, and fraternity. Just in case, right?' (2011: 163). It seems to us that precisely in these 'just in case' or 'as if' rests the essence of the political performative: act 'as if' your act matters, publish 'just in case' a million readers will read you, unlearn everything you know 'just in case' this will open up new sensibilities and patterns of thought, make political art 'as if' it will create political reality.

It is in Berardi's elaboration of reasons for resistance that we find the strongest resonances with *sigma*: his text appears to us, indeed, as *sigmatic*. For in the Italian author's predicament that the political task of the future is the creation of a form of self-consciousness for the presently ignorant general intellect (2011: 163), we identify a resonance with *sigma*'s insurrection of a million minds. And Berardi's invisible insurrection would essentially take place through a novel form of colonisation of the 'grids of expression':

> Poetry and therapy (thera-poetry) will be the forces leading to the creation of a cognitarian self-consciousness: not a political party, not the organization of interests, but the reactivation of the cognitarian sensibility. . . . The new space for activism is here, in the connection of poetry, therapy, and the creation of new paradigms.
>
> (2011: 163)

This new creation of paradigms cannot occur but through a 'just in case' type of thought: that after the end of the future there is hope. Again, Berardi's words, this time from the *Post-Futurist Manifesto*, which would echo the *sigmatic* collaboration and self-organisation, within the spontaneous university of poets, artists, physicists, psychotherapists and neurobiologists: 'We demand that art turns into a life-changing force. We seek to abolish the separation between poetry and mass communication, to reclaim the power of media from the merchants and return it to the poets and the sages' (2011: 166).

Thera-poetry – a *sigmatic* neologism that we would like to use, alongside Berardi, in order to describe the space and temporality for contemporary art activism. It encapsulates the refusal of traditional party politics and the mobilisation of tactics meant to 'seize the grid of expression' that would turn art into a 'life-changing force'.

What we need to retain from *sigma*, however, is that thera-poetry cannot take place unless the individual subject is replaced in its social nexus. Activism as 'living art' is necessarily an 'art of living' within communities, right in the heart of our towns and cities: it is viral, infiltrating and exfiltrating the grids of official culture and politics. The spontaneous university, placed on a river bank outside of London, failed to happen. However, the London Anti-University happened in 1968, as well as myriad independent hubs of militant knowledge that continue to emerge on the globe. And it is here, at the level of strategic alliance, where *sigma* needs to take place: simply because we cannot know what comes after the end of the future, just 'as if' an insurrectionary alliance becomes the future's political realism.

Notes

1 The claim that art activism is 'doing' politics with art is based on Dorothea von Hantelmann's analyses of 'things done with art' (see Hantelmann, 2010).
2 See Alberro and Stimson (2009) for an anthology of programmatic texts offering an understanding of scope and specificity of institutional critique's different 'waves'.
3 In addition to the reading of *sigma* as an offshoot of Situationism International (e.g. Wark 2011; Gardiner, 2006), Gill Tasker (2016) proposes a reading of *sigma* through the lens of existential philosophy.
4 Compare, for example, with the visually rich narratives of Kingsley Hall in Mary Barnes's and Joseph Berke's accounts, in Barnes (1973).
5 There exists a strong resonance with this idea and Félix Guattari's idea of production of subjectivity according a new aesthetic paradigm. See for example Guattari (1995).
6 Compare this with the discussions on the figure of 'exile' emerging from the academic (re)discovery of Deleuze and Guattari.
7 There is a striking resemblance between the project of the spontaneous university and Fourier's *phalanstère* (see Beecher and Bienvenu, 1971), a comparison that we cannot pursue in the present study.
8 In the past decade there has been a renewed interest in 'unlearning' and 'deschooling'. For example, Nora Sternfeld organised a two-year MA programme in Curating, Managing and Mediating Art at Aalto University around these topics (Sternfeld, 2016). In 2010 Serpentine Galleries organised a research conference titled 'Deschooling Society' (Serpentine Galleries, 2010). Noteworthy is Irit Rogoff's insistence on processes of 'unframing' knowledge within the contemporary university (Rogoff, 2010). These themes can be traced back to Paul Goodman and Ivan Illich's ideas as formulated in Goodman (1964) and Illich (1971).

Bibliography

The texts in the *sigma portfolio* (British Library Reference Number HS.74/1373) are individually paginated and separate from each other. There is no overall pagination of the portfolio, so we decided to refer to individual texts within the portfolio in the following way:

> BLU = *sigma: A Tactical Blueprint* (A. Trocchi).
> GEN = *sigma: General Information* (A. Trocchi).
> INV = *Invisible Insurrection of a Million Minds* (A. Trocchi).

Alberro, Alexander, and Blake Stimson, eds. 2009. *Institutional Critique: An Anthology of Artists' Writings*. Cambridge, MA: MIT Press.

Austin, J. L. 1962. *How to Do Things with Words*. Oxford: Clarendon Press.

Barnes, Mary and Joseph Berke. 1973. *Two Accounts of a Journey through Madness*. Harmondsworth: Penguin.

Beecher, Jonathan and Richard Bienvenu, eds. 1971. *The Utopian Vision of Charles Fourier: Selected Texts on Work, Love, and Passionate Attraction*. Boston: Beacon Press.

Berardi, Franco 'Bifo'. 2009. *The Soul at Work: From Alienation to Autonomy*. Translated by Francesca Cadel and Giuseppina Mecchia. Los Angeles, CA: Semiotext(e).

———. 2011. *After the Future*. Edited by Gary Genosko and Nicholas Thoburn. Translated by: Arianna Bove, Melinda Cooper, Erik Empson, Enrico, Giuseppina Mecchia, and Tiziana Terranova. Oakland, CA: AK Press.

Derrida, Jacques. 1988. 'Signature Event Context'. *Limited Inc*. Translated by Samuel Weber and Jeffrey Mehlman. Evanston, IL: Northwestern University Press, 1–24.

Fisher, Mark. 2009. *Capitalist Realism: Is There No Alternative?* Winchester, UK: O Books.

———. 2014. *Ghosts of My Life: Writings on Depression, Hauntology and Lost Futures*. Winchester, UK: Zero Books.

Gardiner, Michael. 2006. *From Trocchi to Trainspotting: Scottish Critical Theory since 1960*. Edinburgh: Edinburgh University Press.

Goodman, Paul. 1964. *Compulsory Miseducation*. 2nd rev ed. Harmondsworth: Penguin Books.

Groys, Boris. 2008. *Art Power*. Cambridge: MIT Press.

Guattari, Félix. 1995. *Chaosmosis: An Ethico-Aesthetic Paradigm*. Translated by Paul Bains and Julian Pefanis. Bloomington, IN: Indiana University Press.

Hantelmann, Dorothea von. 2010. *How to Do Things with Art: The Meaning of Art's Performativity*. Zurich: JRP/Ringier & Les presses du réel.

Horowitz, Michael. 2004. 'Jeff Nuttall. Author of 1968's Bomb Culture'. *The Guardian*, January 12, 2004. Available at: www.theguardian.com/news/2004/jan/12/guardianobituaries.artsobituaries [accessed: 30/04/2018].

Illich, Ivan. 1971. *Deschooling Society*. New York: Harper & Row.

Katz, Vincent, Martin Brody, Robert Creeley, and Kevin Power. 2013. *Black Mountain College: Experiment in Art*. Cambridge, MA: The MIT Press.

Laing, R. D. 1967. *The Politics of Experience*. New York: Pantheon Books.

Laing, R. D. 2010. *The Divided Self. An Existential Study in Sanity and Madness.* [New ed.] London: Penguin.

Lenin, V. I. 1999 (1902). *What Is to Be Done?* (Marxists Internet Archive, available as pdf from; trans. by Joe Fineberg and George Hanna).

Miller, Jason. 2018. 'The Arts and the Liberal Arts at Black Mountain College'. *The Journal of Aesthetic Education* 52 (4): 49–68.

Molesworth, Helen. 2015. *Leap before You Look: Black Mountain College, 1933–1957.* New Haven: Yale University Press.

Nuttall, Jeff. 1968. *Bomb Culture.* London: MacGibbon & Kee.

Osborne, Peter. 2013. *Anywhere or Not at All: Philosophy of Contemporary Art.* London: Verso Books.

Rogoff, Irit. 2010. 'Free'. *E-flux Journal*, #14 – March 2010. Available at: www.e-flux.com/journal/14/61311/free/ [accessed: 15/08/2018].

Searle, John R. 1969. *Speech Acts: An Essay in the Philosophy of Language.* Cambridge: Cambridge University Press

Serpentine Galleries. 2010. *Deschooling Society* (29th April 2010). Available at: www.serpentinegalleries.org/learn/research/conference-deschooling-society [accessed: 15/08/2018].

Sternfeld, Nora. 2016. 'Learning Unlearning'. *CuMMA Papers*, #20. Available at: https://cummastudies.files.wordpress.com/2016/09/cumma-papers-20.pdf [accessed: 15/08/2018].

Tasker, Gill. 2016. 'The Alternative Communities of Alexander Trocchi'. *Community in Modern Scottish Literature.* Edited by Scott Lyall. Leiden: Brill, 124–42.

Trocchi, Alexander. 1960. *Cain's Book.* New York: Grove Press.

———. 1964. *Sigma Portfolio.* London: Project Sigma.

———, and Jeff Nuttall. 1965. *The Moving Times.* London: Moving Times.

Wark, McKenzie. 2011. *The Beach Beneath the Street: The Everyday Life and Glorious Times of the Situationist International.* London: Verso.

Whiteley, Gillian. 2011. 'Sewing the "Subversive Thread of Imagination": Jeff Nuttall, Bomb Culture and the Radical Potential of Affect'. *The Sixties* 4 (2): 109–33.

4 Challenging state-led political violence with art activism

Focus on borders[1]

Amy Corcoran

Introduction

Art activism is a means of changing public perceptions, including perceptions of state violence. Activist-artists advance two arguments: first, that legally sanctioned state actions can still be regarded as violence (and morally reprehensible) and, second, that it is legitimate to resist such violence, even using defensive violence.

Art activists use numerous tactics and methods to convey these ideas. Public acts, for example, manipulate and use public spaces, often those commonly associated with state power, as platforms. They variously employ humour, satire and empathy, putting viewers in other peoples' situations, to encourage audience participation, increase engagement and maximise understanding. However, there is a difference between awareness and comprehension, concern and action. Activist-artists also try to build comprehension and stimulate action. (De)legitimation, education and empathy are particularly important in this respect.

To discuss art activism, I will first explore the concept by outlining its relationship with recent protest actions. I then consider practitioners' conceptions of violence. I argue that violence is not limited to physical acts and that *political* violence can indeed be enacted by states. I contextualise the claim by exploring forms of art activism that challenge European government enforcement of national borders, thus looking at violence as it relates to migration. Third, I apply this conception of political violence to evaluate three processes activist-artists employ to support political struggles. These processes are explored both with reference to concepts of legitimacy and denial originating in political and social theory and in sociological and performance contexts, which focus on the relationship between the artist and their participants or collaborators, as well as the impact of artworks on audiences.

My aim is to show how creative practices link localised actions to global movements, how ideological arguments are made tangible through art actions and how activist-artists are able to adopt a dual position as critics of state violence and advocates of grassroots resistance. The consideration of strategy makes use of tangible examples to theorise potential responses and make recommendations for approaches to art activism that may be more likely to result in productive outcomes. My argument is that art activism supports social transformation and that it occupies an important place in contemporary political struggles.

The concept: creative resistance to state violence

The space for art activism as a discrete strategy or tactic expanded in the 1990s, coinciding with the full-scale roll out of advanced global neoliberal policy (Mayer, 2013) and concurrently – albeit paradoxically – the fortification of national borders (Graeber, 2004). As Alison Jeffers notes, concern that migrant abuse of social security systems encouraged Western governments to 'exercise hostile and increasingly exclusionary legislation to attempt to maintain their borders and minimise disruption on political, social and economic levels' (2011: 148). The hostility was aggravated by the geopolitical situation and fear of terrorism, which escalated dramatically following 9/11: the global 'war on terror' had a significant impact on the securitisation of European borders and internal surveillance (Levi and Wall, 2004). It also triggered significant trans-European migrant solidarity actions, such as campaigns to end detention and close detention centres, often as part of wider campaigns to eliminate immigration controls (Hayter, 2004). In 1997, Kein Mensch Ist Illegal (No One Is Illegal; NOII) was set up. The No Border network followed in 1999 (Walters, 2006; Nail, 2015). Links between pro-migration movements and art became explicit in the formation of NOII, which launched at the international art festival, *documenta X*, led by three German artists.

Intensive civil society resistance to neoliberal globalisation took shape during this period, through mass Summit protests and the emergence of the Global Justice Movement (GJM). The 1999 Seattle World Trade Organization shut-down, the 'Battle for Seattle', was a defining moment, renown for its size, potency and creativity (Flesher Fominaya and Cox, 2013). Indeed, Christian Scholl (2011) argues that the Summit protests encapsulated the creative potential of the time, merging expression and tactics to develop new repertoires of action. Likewise A.K. Thompson celebrates the 'extreme creative audacity' of these years, the plethora of 'tactical innovations' and 'aesthetic interventions' (2011: 35). This process of invention and investigation is what David Graeber calls a 'new language' of civil disobedience, which combines 'elements of street theatre, festival and what can only be called non-violent warfare' (2004: 208).

The space that emerged for art activism was strengthened by simultaneous moves towards direct political action by artists. Art's transgressive potential had been explored by numerous artists and groups in the 1970s to 1990s, such as the Guerrilla Art Action Group, Suzanne Lacy, PAD/D and Group Material (Kester, 1998). Yet while art institutions had begun to embrace activist-art around the turn of the millennium, radical art underwent a shift and ceased looking to the field of art production for validation (Holmes, 2009). Such 'engaged art practices' have been differently described and theorised by Mary Jacob (1995), Miwon Kwon (2002), Claire Bishop (2004) and Grant Kester (2004). As an example of this new framework, Action Terroriste Socialement Acceptable (ATSA), working in Canada in the late 1990s, carried out 'multifaceted activist interventions' in public; Marc James Léger claimed they were representative of the many 'socially engaged' art collectives that formed following the full realisation of the GJM in Seattle (2011: 51). At this point then, artist collectives actively decided to involve themselves directly with political activity, energised by alterglobalisation movements.

Because political art is often labelled 'critical art', Léger terms the output of these collectives as critical public art or critical community art. The category of 'street art' is also thought to have emerged in the late 1990s, partly from an association with alterglobalisation and antiwar movements and the revival of certain ephemeral art mediums re-popularised after the birth of the Internet (MacDowall, 2015: 35). The umbrella term 'cultural activism' is also used to describe these new practices, though Grindon (2011) finds the concept elusive. Yet however they are labelled, these various tactics can be understood to have the general aim of 'disturbing and reorienting the cultural and political sphere' (Firat and Kuryel, 2011: 10). They include sousveillance, media hoaxes, adbusting, subvertising, flash mobs, street art, hacktivism, political performance and billboard liberation (Firat and Kuryel, 2011: 10).

Politically motivated creative actions that intervene in public space are one form of cultural activism: 'art activism' or 'artivism'. The nuances lie in the relationship posited between 'art' and 'activism' and the autonomy of artists. 'Art activism' describes artwork produced for activist purposes yet detached from protest movement activity. It differs from the use of creative tactics within mass protests. Creative political actions that take place outside protests but that are directly related to social movements may also be considered art activism. These tend to be carried out by small 'affinity groups' that are aligned to or members of larger political or social organisations. The acts are often risky or illegal and are frequently done in the name of that organisation, rather in the name of the cause in general. For example, creative actions by members of Greenpeace are *Greenpeace* actions, rather than an activist-artist. Activist-art actions may be aligned with that of Greenpeace and carried out to highlight ecological issues but would be undertaken independently (Boustred, 2016). The activist-artist in this hypothetical case may even be a member of Greenpeace, but the action would not be carried out in Greenpeace's name, with their formal consent and backing (though the organisation may support it informally).

Art activism may also encompass creative and aesthetic actions instigated by individuals who do not self-define as 'artists'. For Firat and Kuryel (2011) this rendering reclaims creativity and imagination from the figure of the artist and the creative class – art activists merge activism, art, politics and performance. In this formulation art activism overlaps with creative direct action, prompting arguments about what constitutes art, specifically in this context and in general. I follow the work of Malcolm Miles (2009) who focuses on the works' impact rather than arguments about the nature of 'art', which are often self-referential and circular. In reality, methods of political engagement, terms and tactics bleed into one another and the similarities turn on the centrality of political motivation to the actions and their use of creativity to convey meaning or messages in a manner that departs from traditional or non-creative civil society action. While these actions exist somewhat separately from protest moments they can continue to be understood as 'activism', rather than as political commentary in gallery spaces, for example.

The context: capitalist crisis and migration

Art activism was reshaped in the wake of the 2008 global financial crisis. While the crisis appeared to reveal the instability of capitalism, it ultimately led to the reinforcement of its economic and political systems as governments pushed through austerity measures that intensified inequality and protected the financial institutions. This had knock-on effects on migration, as governments sought to control spending through exclusion, with irregular migrants also regularly blamed for financial failure and growth in unemployment (Castles, 2011). As normalised state violence became more entrenched, activist-art responded by seeking to expose and challenge state abuses of power.

Jonathan Pugh (2009) notes that the financial crisis and recession not only focused attention equally on the economy and society and the environment. Radical politics shifted towards the articulation of the claims of the excluded or ignored. This was the case in much migration-related campaigning. Indeed, from the outset, the GJM's opposition to corporate global capitalism included core concerns over freedom of movement. As Graeber (2004) argued, neoliberal globalisation promoted freedom of capital and goods and restrictions on labour. It stoked a plethora of creative actions that focused on migration and borders in the early 2000s: individuals dressed up as border guards, the construction of boat-bridges across rivers and airport blockades to protest against deportations, including one with an orchestra. No Border camps were organised across Europe, including one in Strasbourg, selected as the home of the Schengen Information System (Alldred, 2003), a 'search-and-control database with tens of thousands of terminals across Europe, targeting the movements of migrants, activists, anyone they like' (Graeber, 2004: 206).

Migration-related campaigns have become more visible as the large-scale mass movement of peoples exposed the violence involved in contemporary bordering practices. This strand of art activism regularly demonstrates a commitment to supporting struggles by encouraging action and generating new avenues of thought. Activist-artists working across Europe today sometimes direct audiences towards tangible campaigns and sometimes choose not to, favouring more open interpretation of their work. The Hummingbird Project (2015) staged *Pop Up Calais* – a miniature recreation of Calais outside a British town council building – as part of a campaign to urge the local council to accept more refugees. In the same year Public Studio (2015) presented *Migrant Choir*: migrants stuck in Italy sang the French, British and Italian national anthems outside the national pavilions at the Venice Biennale. Information booklets explained the wider situation regarding migration but did not promote any particular campaign or course of action. The intervention was designed to generate an affective encounter in which a feeling of 'home' generated by the anthems jarred with the situations of the singers.

In the following section I explore attempts by art activists to legitimise anti state violence as resistance, as well as activist-art's delegitimation of state-led political violence and consider two methods – education and empathy.

(De)legitimation of violence

Activist groups and activist-artists highlight the physical and structural dimensions of state violence. *Les Misérables*, Banksy's (2016) mural opposite the French embassy in London is an example (Ellis-Petersen, 2016). It depicts the position of irregular migrants in Europe as the contemporary *misérables* of liberal democratic societies, subject to routine structural political violence. Formalising Banksy's imagery, Slavoj Žižek argues that violence is not exhausted by 'subjective' violence – physical actions committed by an actor and incorporating civil unrest – and that it has 'symbolic' and 'systemic' forms (2008: 1–3). Žižek designates this as the 'often catastrophic consequences of the smooth functioning of our economic and political systems'.[2] His view chimes with Gregg Barak's understanding of violence as 'any action or structural arrangement that results in physical or nonphysical harm to one or more persons' (2003: 26). Police brutality and government inaction fall into this bracket (Green and Ward, 2004). State violence also incorporates genocide, capital punishment and torture, war and some of its tactics, such as strategic use of rape (Farwell, 2004).

Charles Tilly (1985) argues that political violence is integral to the state, deployed to protect citizens from each other and from (alleged) external enemies. States claim a monopoly of violence; this is legitimised by public acceptance (Weber, 1919/2015). As David Beetham explains, legitimacy rests on the congruence of a 'system of power' with 'the beliefs, values and expectations that provide its justification' (1991: 11). This is not simply a matter of legal entitlement but the purchase of shared moral or political norms (Green and Ward, 2000). In order for relevant hegemonic notions to proceed without interrogation, the state must be considered legitimate.

Some political theorists (for example, Muller, 1972/2014) argue that state violence thus falls outside the definition of 'political violence'. Yet this conception collapses legitimacy into the reality of the state's monopoly and denies the possibility of challenge. Legal scholar Robert Cover (1986), however, contests this and particularly criticises the reality of the *threat* of state-led violence even when the state does not actually enact it. Thus, taking the treatment of prisoners as his focal point, Cover argues that 'the experience of the prisoner is, from the outset, an experience of being violently dominated, and it is coloured from the beginning by the fear of being violently treated' (1986: 1608). In a similar vein, Walter Benjamin (1921/1996) considered law as violence and domination, referring to the drawing and maintenance of borders as a phenomenon demonstrating state domination and enforcement of future violence. He argued that it is necessary and indeed 'obligatory' to end this pattern of law-making and law-sustaining violence, justifying 'revolutionary violence'. State violence can be challenged. Indeed, this process is vital if abuses of state power are to be minimised.

Art activism is one forum through which state behaviour can be called into question and delegitimised and can be particularly effective as many Western countries continue to experience the crisis of legitimacy that Jürgen Habermas (1976) pointed to forty years ago. In discussions on contemporary migration, Raymond Michalowski (2007) notes this trend in the USA, as does Fran Cetti (2014) looking at the European context. Activist-art's potential here is especially important when the ability to vocalise counter-hegemonic narratives to wider audiences remains significantly impeded. Art can provide a powerful challenge by delegitimising state violation of social norms; visually arresting emotive actions work on different registers to mainstream rhetoric. Realities cannot be ignored or sanitised; we connect and empathise, especially when actions break into public spaces. These creative outputs can simultaneously remind audiences of norms and values held dear, demonstrate governments' neglect or contravention of these values and suggest future directions. Conveying this information visually and emotionally collapses the distance states seek to put between them and the victims of their violence, and instead addresses audiences intuitively. Žižek asserts that humanitarian crises result from symbolic and systemic violence – the kind of violence that usually fails to provoke uproar unless its victims fit a particular profile. Art activism then seeks to correct this, to create uproar and hold the state to account.

Tammam Azzam's (2013) digital recreation of Gustav Klimt's *The Kiss*, one of the most powerful images to come out of Syria since the civil war, depicts physical state violence and the structural forces that fuel it. Presented as a digitally-rendered mural on the side of a bombed-out building (Jones, 2013), the lovers embrace, their golden moment disintegrating as we see through them into the apartments behind; the windows gone, walls punctured with holes, laundry left hanging. The image has a grace that is at complete odds with its bloody canvas. Set in this new context, the painting becomes a plea for peace and a demand that the world take notice of the Syrian people's plight. Azzam explains: 'I chose it as an icon of love, a way of looking for the stories of love behind this wall that was completely obliterated by the machinery of war'. There is also a strong critique in Azzam's selections, as he actively chooses Western masterpieces to 'draw attention to the tragedy of Syria' and remind Westerners that 'we are all citizens of the same world' and that 'empathy should not be limited to the first world' (Azzam, quoted in, Wyatt, 2015).

The echoes of state-led physical violence are apparent across the image, but the structural reasons behind this violence are clear from the digital mural's context and made plain by Azzam himself. This conception of state-led political violence, expressed through art activism, aligns with arguments advanced in global justice movements since the 1990s. It powerfully renders ideological and political arguments tangible, as well as the outcomes of politically-motivated state abuses.

The promotion of protests and uprisings is another aspect of art activist delegitimation. Here, art activism depicts imagery from non-violent disobedience, such as practiced as part of and in response to Occupy. Art also featured heavily in the student-led Umbrella Revolution, which emerged from protests against proposed changes to electoral processes in Hong Kong in 2014. While a great deal of the creative output was digital and iconographic, the main occupation site, which became known as Umbrella

Square, also played host to numerous installations, sculptures and participatory creative actions. These often reflected the aims of the movement or the people active in it, such as the *Umbrella Man*, a twelve-foot sculpture representing a protestor using an umbrella to shield themselves from tear gas (Dipshan, 2015). Similarly, Demerdash (2012) argues that political murals, often created anonymously in Egypt and Tunisia during the Arab Spring, assumed a great significance. Art works can also visually reference full-scale revolutionary behaviour, which at times employs forms of subjective violence or aggression. This is done to legitimise this behaviour and demonstrate its necessity or justification due to the aggression and provocation of state(s), i.e. to delegitimise the actions of the state. An anonymous mural in Iraqi Kurdistan appearing in advance of the non-binding referendum on Kurdish Independence in 2017 and depicting Kurdish freedom fighters on horseback, was another such visual representation (Chmaytelli and Georgy, 2017). These acts of political violence can be considered manifestations of what Tilly and Tarrow (2015) call 'contentious politics' or the politically-driven use of disruptive tactics. This places the actions of artists in opposition to state practice and acknowledges their disruptive nature while also recognising the minimal physical harm they inflict, compared to other forms of contentious politics.

The legitimation of state violence considered in terms of its Weberian logic draws particular attention to the structural violence involved in bordering. Michalowski (2007) argues that hegemonic narratives equate borders with a strong state that keeps citizens safe. Thus the US government tries to bolster its legitimacy by constructing a wall to meet a conjured external threat from which it can 'protect' its citizens, as well as using migrants as scapegoats for the country's economic problems. More generally, state violence is manifested in behaviours towards irregular migrants by European governments – both before and after they reach European shores (Razum and Bozorgmehr, 2015). Examples include the excessive use of immigration detention, immigration raids and strategies of 'non-arrival', which includes bilateral agreements with a 'circle of friends' – including Morocco and Libya – to prevent unauthorised arrivals and facilitate forced returns (Weber, 2010: 36). In 'Dossiers of Violence', Calais Migrant Solidarity (2014) documents incidences of subjective violence against migrants in Calais used by both French and British states. States also construct images of the migrant 'other' and 'outsiders inside': threats not only to national security but national identity, too, thereby justifying the expansion and deepening of surveillance and systems of exclusion (Aas, 2011; Weber, 2010).

Stanley Cohen's (2001) seminal work on denial demonstrates the plethora of strategies states employ to neutralise and distance themselves from actions that compromise political legitimacy. These include fear-mongering, the 'denial of the victim' and 'condemning the condemners' to delegitimise those involved in resistance. Art activism can counter by sending its messages to wider audiences in new registers.

The violence involved in the return of individuals to sites of persecution, war or poverty is the focus of work by long-time collaborators Peter Kennard and Cat Phillipps. Aligned with various social movements for many decades, Kennard and Phillipps often produce artwork for campaign materials and protests. Their photomontage image *In Humanity* (2016), for example, depicts a small inflatable dinghy of refugees floating through the ruins of a Syrian city to convey the realities of government policies by visually returning refugees to the warzone they have fled.

Similarly, in the face of intimidation by the French authorities towards volunteers working in the Calais 'Jungle', Jeta Bejtullahu (2015) developed her *Be In Their Shoes* project to not only encourage empathy for and solidarity with migrants stuck in Calais but also for the volunteers supporting them. The images of a muddy footprint along with the campaign's title were spray-painted around Brighton, UK, the hashtag directing people to the campaign's website, which informed people on the situation in Calais. Political violence enacted by states in the pursuit of border control does not simply focus on those the state wishes to keep outside its territory but extends to its own citizens who work against its policy aims.

To conclude this section: states are constituted and maintained by violence and justify the use of this violence in various ways. This violence is not always recognised as such because of the success of strategies such as denial and the power of legal codes (Green and Ward, 2012). Art activism gives voice to narratives that counter those propagated by government or mainstream media, or that are hidden from discourse.[3] Activist-artists use their particular skills to align themselves with and advance these struggles. Their work may initially appear strange within the realm of political action. However, these public representations present an alternative to government rhetoric and divert attention back to the protesters' perspectives, thereby also presenting their actions in a positive light. Artists may be involved in traditional activism. Conversely, they may choose to lend their support to these movements solely through creative action and may not even identify as activists at all. Numerous challenges and limitations confront traditional methods of protest and counter-cultural political communication in contemporary Western societies (Irzik, 2011). Susan Haedicke (2013) therefore argues that direct political action in public spaces may be the only way to engage in unmediated communication with strangers and to reach the media. However, activist-artists must attend to their choices because, while controversial actions have the potential to throw government practice into sharp relief, there is a risk, too, that reactions will centre on this controversy and not the message that activist-artists seek to convey.

Education: making denial undeniable

Educative work and 'awareness raising' presents a serious challenge for artists: how does one present complex ideas in a manner that is accessible to those who are not 'in the know' – both in terms of the art world and politics? Accessibility is key here, and it can determine whether an action engages a broad ensemble of individuals or only manages to fascinate academic and artistic circles. Interpretation is central to this process; reimagining situations in ways that are relatable and significant can become the trigger that sparks understanding beyond mere comprehension of facts and figures. This may then encourage those latter outcomes – concern and action.[4] The various strategies employed within art activism therefore often have similar underlying core concerns: to permit the viewer to appreciate a complex political situation in such a way that new understandings are generated – understandings that will hopefully lead to concrete action. This is seen with *Migrant Choir* by Public Studio, discussed earlier, where a combination of an emotive action reliant on a familiar ritual – singing national anthems – provided a 'way in' to the realities of contemporary bordering practices.

Artists who work to strengthen opposition to inhumane practices by demonstrating the violence of border control practices sometimes try to force the public to embody experiences of violence. Núria Güell's (2013) extended *Too Much Melanin* project employed a political asylum seeker in Sweden to play 'hide and seek' with passers-by. While initiating this, the asylum seeker explained her reasons for leaving her home country and the way she was treated in Sweden, which included real-life and high-risk games of 'hide and seek' with the Swedish police. Güell sought to fabricate an excuse for Swedish citizens to interact with an asylum seeker and to hear the story of her treatment by the Swedish state direct from her. Through this project, the asylum-seeking participant became a three-dimensional person whose motivations and needs were understood, and the structural violence of the state was also laid bare.

For political violence enacted by the state to be understood as such, activist-artists must uncover and cut through tactics of denial, dehumanisation and neutralisation, something Güell goes some way towards. Yet art activism has to do more than paint terrible situations as unfortunate tragedies because the state separates itself from its actions in ingenious ways. This is often supported by sections of the media, as was seen in the aftermath of Alan Kurdi's death, the young boy whose body was found washed up on a Turkish beach. Soon after the photos of Kurdi's body made global headlines, his father, Abdullah Kurdi, was either blamed outright for his son's death or had his credibility as a refugee called into question (Powell and Weise, 2015).[5]

Activist-artists may respond to specific manifestation of political violence, such as deaths within detention centres, not only to highlight this incidence but also to challenge the legitimacy of the entire border control regime. The Berlin-based Center for Political Beauty (CPB) addressed this conjunction in multiple actions. In *Eating Refugees* (2016), CPB highlighted the practice of outsourcing border controls to airlines by enforcing the need for visas, preventing migrants from reaching European countries to claim asylum without using life-threatening 'illegal' means. It also referenced the EU-Turkey deal, through which migrants would be detained and deported from Turkey before reaching the EU. The action included a Syrian actress giving a public speech to say that she would be willing to be eaten by tigers (two tigers were located in an enclosure in a Berlin public square for this performance) unless the regulations were changed. While this was a performance and not a genuine threat (she did not give herself up to be eaten when the Air Berlin flight CPB chartered from Turkey to Germany was cancelled), it drew attention to the German state complicity in a life or death matter. The action involved a very public condemnation of legislation enforcing these practices, which ultimately led to CPB filing a lawsuit against the German government claiming that this legislation is unconstitutional (Center for Political Beauty, 2016).

In 2014, CPB carried out *First Fall of the European Wall*, which sought to demonstrate the hypocrisy of celebrating the fall of one wall while fortifying another (Center for Political Beauty, 2014). As part of this project, the group stole white crosses, which made up part of Berlin's celebrations marking the twenty-fifth anniversary of the Berlin Wall's destruction. They took these to the border fences on the outskirts of Europe and photographed migrants holding them, before positioning them on the fences. The action's controversial nature sparked strong reactions. The inclusion of migrants within the project and the direct link between Germany's intimate history with separation walls and its current position as a central force in contemporary 'Fortress Europe' sought to render these temporal connections salient. Collapsing time in this way was an attempt to lay out these double standards in a comprehensible way, to encourage a reconsideration of contemporary bordering practices and to understand that situations change – Germans actively seek to move away from Germany's recent histories, will they look back at this new border fence with shame in the future?

This project demonstrates why art activism must tread a delicate line between generating interest and controversy. Different audiences will respond differently to actions, so activists must consider this when formulating and situating their interventions. Actions can easily infuriate certain groups and increase animosity towards refugees. For example, Manaf Halbouni's (2017) *Monument*, an installation of three upturned buses positioned in Dresden's central square where the far-right group Pegida regularly gather for demonstrations, referenced a well-known image from Aleppo, Syria where a community had positioned three bombed-out buses as a barricade. The unveiling was met with protests by right-wingers who claimed the installation represented an abuse of artistic freedom and a 'snub' to the views of Dresden residents (Oltermann, 2017). Ultimately, the levels of global coverage and discussion generated, as well as the presentation of Dresden as a hotbed for far-right sentiment, suggests that the risk that Halbouni's installation would backfire was worth taking, and indeed it was re-commissioned for display in Berlin. However, *Monument*'s impact on different factions in Dresden is likely to be complex and perhaps negative.

Humour can also be deployed to render situations farcical and cast new light on them. *Please Love Austria*, a 2000 action by Christoph Schlingensief, invited the public to vote to deport or save asylum seekers through a week-long reality TV style performance (Schlingensief, 2000). Drawing intense interest and protests from all sides of the political spectrum, the phony TV show made a mockery of the xenophobia it drew out of Austrian citizens. Another notable satirical project, *Deportation Class* (2000), led by group of No One Is Illegal activists, ultimately forced Lufthansa to cease deportations on commercial flights and inspired the refusal of paying passengers to sit down while a deportee was on board. Although the state responded by deporting individuals on privately chartered flights, the action provides a useful example of censure and informal sanction. Boycotts, too, can act as powerful sanctions, and this is perhaps where art activism and more traditional civil society organising can provide a mutually supportive relationship – to reach new audiences and provide a base for concrete action.

In the West, art activism does not need to direct its efforts entirely on exposé since many individuals have access to information through the Internet and other media sources – albeit often warped and partial.[6] It can also focus on the rhetorical power of labelling state violence as *violence* and state crimes as *crimes*. Strengthening censure and sanction is vital to resistance here, and this in part achieved through the creation of counter-hegemonic arguments and education, often considered 'awareness raising'. This is no easy feat; the images we are daily bombarded with can make us numb and immune to pleas and facts. To break through this, realities must be presented in a manner that goes beyond factual narrative and to trigger affect and empathy.

Empathy: tactics of re-humanisation

Where states neutralise and dehumanise, art activism 'rehumanises'. It punctures narratives formulated around the 'other' and exposes the violence of actions taken against them. Increasing the salience of victims helps to counter governments' exclusionary processes (Weber, 2010). Leanne Weber and Sharon Pickering (2011) thus argue that accounts of border deaths must also lament the loss of individual human beings. Such an attempt was coordinated by Snappin' Turtle Productions (2016), who laid out over 2,500 used lifejackets outside London's Parliament Square to represent recent deaths of migrants travelling to Europe. Many of the lifejackets had belonged to children and were personalised. They were laid out uniformly on the square as a graveyard, and refugees located in the UK were present to discuss their stories with the media. Timed to coincide with the first ever UN Summit for Refugees and Migrants, *Lifejacket London* gained worldwide coverage.

The Dutch group Power of Art House (2015) also highlighted personal stories to focus on individuals rather than faceless 'refugees'. In *Moving People*, thousands of tiny, fragile 3D-printed models of refugees were positioned throughout Amsterdam and The Hague to be discovered. Once found, the refugees' stories could be uncovered through a web-link printed on the figurine. The group statement on the website read:

> Power of Art House wants to give these stories, these people, a human face. By telling their stories and opening eyes. Making connections and showing people a different way of looking at refugees. Encouraging empathy and strengthening social cohesion. Not to blame or shame or judge, but to show the human suffering in the stories of each and every refugee.
>
> (Power of Art House, 2015)

The response was largely positive, and the project made its way onto numerous national and international media outlets, and it has since been re-commissioned for Belgium and America. Yet it begs a question about the distinction between pity and empathy. Heightened levels of victimhood ensure an emotional response, and many have asserted the power of affect instilled through creative means (see, for example, Deleuze and Guattari, 1988). However, when the construction of two-dimensional personas does not relate to the true story, it cannot support genuine connection. In fact, it can create a damaging image of 'deserving' refugees and those who do not fit the accepted pattern, something irregular migrants who go through the asylum process already face when forced to account for themselves to the Home Office. Verbatim theatre has been criticised for failing to consider power dynamics, as have Refugee Festivals for the manner in which they rely on certain representations and depictions of 'refugee-ness' (Jeffers, 2011). Similarly, Banksy was told to 'go home' by a Palestinian man when he went to Gaza to paint murals on the separation wall; they did not want a more beautiful wall, they wanted it gone (Jones, 2005).

Bearing in mind Michel Foucault's warnings about the 'indignity' of speaking for others (1977: 209), it may be argued that artists should avoid representing others. However, as Sue Wilkinson and Celia Kitzinger contend, only speaking for oneself may also lead to disempowerment; for as no one speaks for Others they remain disbarred from mainstream debates, silenced and marginalised. The issue for an artist is how to challenge structural power, while recognising the 'multiple intersecting forms of power and powerlessness; how to think about our own and/or others' Otherness without fixing it as an essential attribute; how to speak without our words serving to disempower Others; and when to remain silent' (Wilkinson and Kitzinger, 2009: 90).

Helen Nicholson suggests that artists should 'create spaces and places which enable voices to be heard' (2014: 163). In theatre, one common tactic is documentary or verbatim performance (Gilbert and Lo, 2007: 191). Examples include *Citizen X* (2002) in Australia by Sidetrack Performance Group (2003), which focused on extracts from letters by detained asylum seekers as a 'quiet ethical form of activism' (Burvill, 2008: 238). In the UK, Banner Theatre (2008) used 'actuality' in the form of video footage in *They Get Free Mobiles . . . Don't They? The Bogus Woman* by Kay Adshead (2001) was based on the testimony of a torture victim. The test here is not to downplay complexities or promote empathy by presenting refugees as saintly characters or victims. Jeffers terms this 'bureaucratic performance' in which the 'right' kind of story must be told (2011: 109). Simplifications risk creating images of victims in the minds of audiences or even in the refugees themselves or reinforce negative attitudes about the countries from which these individuals have fled. But there are other pressures connected with the need for financial support. In bringing these stories into public arenas, artists can find themselves embroiled within restrictive structures connected to the powers and institutions being criticised (Schininà, 2004).

In seeking to effect affect, activist-artists may choose to reconstruct the violence that others are forced to experience. In Brussels and as part of a wider *Frontexit* (2013, emphasis added) campaign, Nimis Groupe performed hoax immigration identity checks on people arriving to work at the EU offices, in order to make these processes visible and demonstrate their violence and proximity. *The Container*, an immersive performance by Clare Bayley (2007) held in a shipping container, permitted visitors to experience something similar to the journeys that many migrants are forced to take.

This strategy puts audiences in the shoes of those who experience violence. It is criticised for its inability to be a *true* reflection of the situation – the participants know the Home Office is not interrogating them even in the midst of the performance (Jeffers, 2011). However, it seems that emotional links, empathy and embodiment of the violence provide routes to develop connections and understandings capable of engendering action. This approach is reminiscent of Augusto Boal's (1979) Theatre of the Oppressed. Boal believed in the power of rehearsing for revolution. Enacting one's ambitions in a theatre environment helped instigate real life political action. The recreations are mere shadows of the true experiences but open up pathways to new perspectives for those who experience them.

Some activist-artists choose to reconstruct violence to lay bare realities without room for distanciation to take place. The QR Code embedded in Banksy's *Les Misérables* facilitated direct communication by enabling viewers with smartphones to view the violence enacted by French police against residents of the Calais 'Jungle' (Horton, 2016). This direct experience, so out of context with its grand surroundings in London, can generate an affective response, more so than the witty mural that it accompanies.[7] Jacques Rancière (2010) notes that there is no direct link between knowledge of a situation and political action. It may be, however, that the inducement of affect could provide something of a much-needed bridge in this regard. In this vein, Feisal Mohamed advocates a 'turn to poignancy' as a way in which we might 'imagine human others in their physical and spiritual dynamics' and which might lead to ethical action 'while seeking to dispense with the privilege of acculturation' (2010: 144, 147).

Public art interventions can incorporate strategies that are 'uncomfortable, disturbing or controversial' to stimulate affective responses (Haedicke, 2013: 127). The audience may be startled into a realisation of their own attitudes through being forced to act (either as the outsider or in reaction to an outsider) and then to critically reflect. The audience's engagement with performed thoughts and feelings is empathetic, embedding 'the experience of Otherness in the spectator's body' (Haedicke, 2013: 140). Bearing witness becomes a live, participatory process (Taylor, 2003).

A similar notion of bearing witness can be achieved through static installation. Like *Lifejacket London*, Ai Weiwei's 2016 Berlin installation of used life jackets is of note (Sierzputowski, 2016). Migrants' presence and simultaneous absence in the space is chilling; witnesses are left to question the desperate attempts people have made to try to make it to where they stand. This question remains unresolved, and the uneasiness engenders an emotional response in those who view it in the heart of a cultural capital. Whether instilling uneasiness leads to positive action and solidifies personal denial is difficult to determine. As discussed earlier in relation to pity, there is a fine line between empathy and guilt. Joseph Slaughter (2010) writes about art providing 'narrative conjunctions' between parallel worlds of pain and pleasure. The question is whether people understand that some flourish while others suffer or some flourish *because* others suffer; can art show us that we are implicated in these systems? Art's telling of our implication extends to our non-telling elsewhere.

The timing of Weiwei's Konzerthaus installation in 2016, after events in Cologne captured the negative mood towards migrants in Germany, is noteworthy. Reports that refugees had been attacking German women celebrating on New Year's Eve (Huggler, 2016) centred on immigration. Official reports did not confirm the involvement of recent migrants, but the far-right capitalised on the opportunity to demonise them. Weiwei's installation of thousands of used lifejackets brought attention back to the issue at hand at a time when attitudes towards migrants were hostile. It remains unclear whether the work encouraged understanding of the state's role in these violent deaths or the public's own complicity. Overall, however, the art activist approach to civil society censure and sanction of state-led political violence aims to link back to government and would be apparent to at least some of those who experience these interventions.

Conclusion

Art activism is an aspect of civil society action against state violence. The artist both aims to censure and enact an informal sanction against the state, while simultaneously bringing into public view the illegitimacy and criminality of state actions. In the case of migration there is also (often) a significant aspiration to work against processes of othering and dehumanisation. Art activism is not didactic but uses myriad engaging methods to reformulate the context, the situation, the state, the 'victims' and even the audiences

Three main strategies have been discussed: (de)legitimation, education (incorporating censure and sanction) and empathy or emotional connection.[8] These are powerful tactics in the toolbox of the activist-artist, and public art interventions appear uniquely placed to bring education and empathy into alignment to produce transformations. Artists are skilled in expression, and art activist public works are less likely to be compromised by bureaucratic ties. Visual communication that speaks to emotion is primed to generate intuitive connection, and those located in the streets are positioned for encounters with a variety of people.

As has been noted throughout the chapter, there are nuances that must be considered when formulating these interventions, which impact both on the outcome of the project and how it is experienced by those it intends to act in solidarity with. These actions have an important role to play in resistance against stated-led violence. However, they form part of the complicated fabric of contemporary civil society mobilisations. In moving beyond the boundaries of fine art and even political or critical art, art activism walks a line between politics and aesthetics. This unique positioning and agility is the source of art activism's strength.

Notes

1 This work was supported by the Economic and Social Research Council [grant number ES/J500124/1].
2 A detailed consideration of the nature and definition of violence is unfortunately beyond the scope of this chapter.
3 This is not to say that activist-artists are not themselves also subject to power relations, biases, agency and hegemony. Art is subject to the same follies as other fields, although its acknowledgement of its own artifice may provide a buffer.
4 At times, presentation of facts can be effective, such as a 2015 action within the EU parliament buildings in which a list of names of the 17,000 people who had died trying to reach Europe between 1990–2012 was laid out on the floor (Nerdcore, 2015).
5 Ai Weiwei's response to Alan Kurdi's death, to recreate the image with the artist taking the position of Kurdi, has been greatly criticised.
6 This is certainly not to say that education and exposé are not important. As discussed previously, governments are adept at hiding practices from citizens that, if uncovered, could lead to their delegitimation.
7 The authorities' response to this mural is also notable. While authorities protect Banksy's pieces that critique capitalism, this was removed within two days of its appearance.
8 The previous have been delineated in reference to irregular migration, but it is contended that general principles can be uncovered that translate to campaigns targeting and resisting other forms of state political violence.

Bibliography

Aas, K. F. 2011. 'Crimmigrant' Bodies and Bona Fide Travelers: Surveillance, Citizenship and Global Governance. *Theoretical Criminology*, 15, 331–46.

Adshead, K. 2001. *The Bogus Woman*. London: Oberon.

Alldred, P. 2003. No Borders, No Nations, No Deportations. *Feminist Review*, 152–7.

Banner Theatre. 2008. *They get free mobiles . . . don't they?* [Online]. Available at https://bannertheatre.co.uk/portfolio/they-get-free-mobiles-dont-they-2008/ [Accessed 2 July 2018].

Barak, G. 2003. *Violence and Nonviolence: Pathways to Understanding*. Thousand Oaks; London: Sage.

Bayley, C. 2007. *The Container*. London: Nick Hern.

Beetham, D. 1991. *The Legitimation of Power*. Basingstoke: Macmillan.

Bejtullahu, J. 2015. Be in Their Shoes [Online]. *jetabejtullahu.com*. Available: www.jetabejtullahu.com/campaigns.html [accessed 2 July 2018].

Benjamin, W. 1921/1996. Critique of Violence. *In:* Bullock, M. P. and Jennings, M. W. (eds.) *Walter Benjamin: Selected Writings.* Cambridge, MA; London: Belknap Press of Harvard University Press.

Bishop, C. 2004. Antagonism and Relational Aesthetics. *October*, 51–79.

Boal, A. 1979. *Theatre of the Oppressed.* London: Pluto Press.

Boustred, H. 2016. Six Greenpeace Non Violent Direct Actions [Online]. *Greenpeace.* Available: www.greenpeace.org.uk/groups/spotlight/six-actions [accessed 7 February 2017].

Burvill, T. 2008. 'Politics Begins as Ethics': Levinasian Ethics and Australian Performance Concerning Refugees. *Research in Drama Education: The Journal of Applied Theatre and Performance*, 13, 233–43.

Calais Migrant Solidarity. 2014. Dossiers of Violence [Online]. *Calais Migrant Solidarity.* Available: https://calaismigrantsolidarity.wordpress.com/videos-and-articles-2/this-border-kills-our-dossier-of-violence/ [accessed 17 November 2018].

Castles, S. 2011. Migration, Crisis, and the Global Labour Market. *Globalizations*, 8, 311–24.

Center for Political Beauty. 2014. *First Fall of the European Wall* [Online]. Available: www.politicalbeauty.com/wall.html [accessed 15 November 2018].

Center for Political Beauty. 2016. *Eating Refugees* [Online]. Available: www.politicalbeauty.com/eatingrefugees.html [accessed 15 November 2018].

Cetti, F. 2014. Border Controls in Europe: Policies and Practices Outside the Law. *State Crime Journal*, 3, 4–28.

Chmaytelli, M. and Georgy, M. 2017. Iraqi Kurds Shrug Off Threats to Hold Independence Vote [Online]. *The Indian Express.* Available: https://indianexpress.com/article/world/iraqi-kurds-shrug-off-threats-to-hold-independence-vote-4860658/ [accessed 17 November 2018].

Cohen, S. 2001. *States of Denial: Knowing about Atrocities and Suffering.* Cambridge; Malden, MA: Polity Press; Blackwell Publishers.

Cover, R. M. 1986. Violence and the Word [Online]. *Faculty Scholarship Series*, 2708. Available: http://digitalcommons.law.yale.edu/fss_papers/2708.

Deleuze, G. and Guattari, F. L. 1988. *A Thousand Plateaus: Capitalism and Schizophrenia.* London: Athlone.

Demerdash, N. 2012. Consuming Revolution: Ethics, Art, and Ambivalence in the Arab Spring. *New Middle Eastern Studies*, 2, Online Journal.

Dipshan, R. 2015. The Art of Hong Kong's Umbrella Revolution [Online]. *The Absolute.* Available: http://theabsolutemag.com/22368/longreads/the-art-of-hong-kongs-umbrella-revolution/ [accessed 17 November 2018].

Ellis-Petersen, H. 2016. Banksy's New Artwork Criticises Use of Teargas in Calais Refugee Camp. *The Guardian*, 24 January 2016.

Farwell, N. 2004. War Rape: New Conceptualizations and Responses. *Affilia*, 19, 389–403.

Firat, B. M. O. Z. and Kuryel, A. 2011. *Cultural Activism: Practices, Dilemmas, and Possibilities.* Amsterdam: Rodopi.

Flesher Fominaya, C. and Cox, L. 2013. *Understanding European Movements: New Social Movements, Global Justice Struggles, Anti-Austerity Protest.* London: Routledge.

Foucault, M. and Deleuze, G. 1977. Intellectuals and Power: A Conversation between Michel Foucault and Gilles Deleuze. *In:* Foucault, M. (ed.) *Language, counter-memory, practice: selected essays and interviews.* Ithaca: Cornell University Press.

Frontexit. 2013. 20th March: The Photos of the Launch [Online]. *frontexit.org.* Available: www.frontexit.org/en/news/item/29-20th-march-the-photos-of-the-launch [accessed 1 July 2018].

Gilbert, H. and Lo, J. 2007. *Performance and Cosmopolitics: Cross-Cultural Transactions in Australasia.* Basingstoke; New York: Palgrave Macmillan.

Graeber, D. 2004. The New Anarchists. *In:* Mertes, T. (ed.) *A Movement of Movements: Is Another World Really Possible?* London; New York: Verso.

Green, P. and Ward, T. 2000. State Crime, Human Rights, and the Limits of Criminology. *Social Justice*, 27, 101–15.

Green, P. and Ward, T. 2004. *State Crime: Governments, Violence and Corruption.* London; Sterling, VA: Pluto Press.

Green, P. and Ward, T. 2012. State Crime: A Dialectical View. *In:* Maguire, M., Morgan, R. and Reiner, R. (eds.) *The Oxford Handbook of Criminology.* 5th ed. Oxford: Oxford University Press.

Grindon, G. 2011. The Notion of Irony in Cultural Activism. *In:* Firat, B. M. O. Z. and Kuryel, A. (eds.) *Cultural Activism: Practices, Dilemmas, and Possibilities.* Amsterdam: Rodopi.

Güell, N. 2013. *Too Much Melanin* [Online]. Available: www.nuriaguell.net/ [accessed 1 July 2018].

Habermas, J. 1976. *Legitimation Crisis.* London: Heinneman Educational Books.

Haedicke, S. C. 2013. *Contemporary Street Arts in Europe: Aesthetics and Politics.* Basingstoke; New York: Palgrave Macmillan.

Halbouni, M. 2017. Art Installation "Monument" 2017 [Online]. *Dresden: manaf-halbouni.com.* Available: www.manaf-halbouni.com/work/monument/ [accessed 3 November 2017].

Hayter, T. 2004. *Open Borders: The Case Against Immigration Controls.* London; Ann Arbor, MI: Pluto Press.

Holmes, B. 2009. Extradisciplinary Investigations: Towards a New Critique of Institutions. *In:* Holmes, B. (ed.) *Escape the Overcode: Activist Art in the Control Society.* Eindhoven: Van Abbemuseum.

Horton, H. 2016. Banksy's 'Les Misérables' Artwork Outside French Embassy in London Criticises Use of Tear Gas at Refugee Camp. *The Telegraph*, 26th January 2016.

Huggler, J. 2016. Cologne New Year Sex Attacks: Germany's Women Are Angry, Scared – And Getting Tired of Excuses. *The Telegraph*, 8th January 2016.

The Hummingbird Project. 2015. Hummingbirds 'Pop up Calais', Brighton and Hove City Council [Online]. *Facebook.* Available: www.facebook.com/Hummingbirduk/posts/984019464973504 [accessed 3 November 2017].

Irzik, E. 2011. A Proposal for Grounded Cultural Activism: Communication Strategies, Adbusters and Social Change. *In:* Firat, B. M. O. Z. and Kuryel, A. (eds.) *Cultural Activism: Practices, Dilemmas, and Possibilities.* Amsterdam: Rodopi.

Jacob, M. J. 1995. *Culture in Action: A Public Art Program of Sculpture Chicago.* Seattle: Bay Press.

Jeffers, A. 2011. *Refugees, Theatre and Crisis: Performing Global Identities*. Basingstoke: Palgrave Macmillan.

Jones, J. 2013. Tammam Azzam's Kiss: An Unromantic Commentary on the Syrian Conflict. *The Guardian*, 4th February 2013.

Jones, S. 2005. Spray Can Prankster Tackles Israel's Security Barrier. *The Guardian*, 5th August 2005.

Kennardphillipps. 2016. In Humanity [Online]. *kennardphillipps.com*. Available: www.kennardphillipps.com/in-humanity-2016/ [accessed 20 January 2019].

Kester, G. H. 1998. *Art, Activism, and Oppositionality: Essays from Afterimage*. Durham, NC; London: Duke University Press.

Kester, G. H. 2004. *Conversation Pieces: Community and Communication in Modern Art*. Berkeley: University of California Press.

Kwon, M. 2002. *One Place After Another: Site Specific Art and Locational Identity*. Cambridge, MA; London: MIT Press.

Léger, M. J. 2011. Afterthoughts on Engaged Art Practice: ATSA and the State of Emergency. *Art Journal*, 70, 50–65.

Levi, M. and Wall, D. S. 2004. Technologies, Security, and Privacy in the Post-9/11 European Information Society. *Journal of Law and Society*, 31, 194–220.

Macdowall, L. 2015. Graffiti, Street Art and Theories of Stigmergy. *In:* Lossau, J. and Stevens, Q. (eds.) *The Uses of Art in Public Space*. New York: Routledge.

Mayer, M. 2013. First World Urban Activism. *City*, 17, 5–19.

Michalowski, R. 2007. Border Militarization and Migrant Suffering: A Case of Transnational Social Injury. *Social Justice*, 34, 62–76.

Miles, M. 2009. Aesthetics in a Time of Emergency. *Third Text*, 23, 421–33.

Mohamed, F. G. 2010. Poignancy as Human Rights Aesthetic. *Journal of Human Rights*, 9, 143–60.

Muller, E. N. 1972/2014. A Test of a Partial Theory of Potential for Political Violence. *American Political Science Review*, 66, 928–59.

Nail, T. 2015. Alain Badiou and the Sans-Papiers. *Angelaki*, 20, 109–30.

Nerdcore. 2015. Names of Drowned Refugees form Walk of Shame on EU-Parliament-Floor [Online]. *Nerdcore.de*. Available: www.nerdcore.de/2015/04/30/names-of-drunk-refugees-for-walk-of-shame-on-eu-parliament-floor/ [accessed 1 July 2018].

Nicholson, H. 2014. *Applied Drama: The Gift of Theatre*. Basingstoke; New York: Palgrave Macmillan.

No One Is Illegal. 2000. "No One Is Illegal" Network Will Not Be Intimidated [Online]. *noborder.org* [accessed 10 December 2017].

Oltermann, P. 2017. Dresden's Bitter Divide Over Aleppo-inspired Bus Barricade Sculpture. *The Guardian*, 7th February 2017.

Powell, M. and Weise, Z. 2015. Aylan and His Father's REAL Story: Abdullah Kurdi Forced to Deny being a Smuggler after New Questions Emerge from Picture that Shook the World [Online]. *Mail Online*. Available: www.dailymail.co.uk/news/article-3232251/Aylan-father-s-REAL-story-Abdullah-Kurdi-forced-deny-smuggler-new-questions-emerge-picture-shook-world.html [accessed 3 July 2018].

Power of Art House. 2015. Moving People [Online]. *power-of-art.nl*. Available: www.power-of-art.nl/campaigns/moving-people/?lang=en [accessed 2nd July 2018].

Public Studio. 2015. Migrant Choir [Online]. *publicstudio.ca*. Available: www.publicstudio.ca/migrant-choir/ [accessed 15 October 2018].

Pugh, J. 2009. *What Is Radical Politics Today?* Basingstoke: Palgrave Macmillan.

Rancière, J. 2010. *Dissensus: On Politics and Aesthetics*. London; New York: Continuum.

Razum, O. and Bozorgmehr, K. 2015. Disgrace at EU's External Borders. *International Journal of Public Health*, 60, 515–16.

Schininà, G. 2004. Here We Are: Social Theatre and Some Open Questions About Its Developments. *TDR: The Drama Review*, 43, 17–31.

Schlingensief, C. 2000. Please Love Austria – First Austrian Coalition Week [Online]. *Schlingensief.com*. Available: www.schlingensief.com/projekt_eng. php?id=t033 [accessed 1 July 2018].

Scholl, C. 2011. Bakunin's Poor Cousins: Engaging Art for Tactical Interventions. *In:* Firat, B. M. O. Z. and Kuryel, A. (eds.) *Cultural Activism: Practices, Dilemmas, and Possibilities*. Amsterdam: Rodopi.

Sidetrack Performance Group. 2003. *Citizen X*. Australasian Drama Studies, 42, 31–56.

Sierzputowski, K. 2016. Ai Weiwei Wraps the Columns of Berlin's Konzerthaus with 14,000 Salvaged Refugee Life Vests [Online]. *This is Colossal*. Available: www.thisiscolossal.com/2016/02/ai-weiwei-konzerthaus-refugee-life-vests/ [accessed 1 July 2018].

Slaughter, J. R. 2010. Vanishing Points: When Narrative Is Not Simply There. *Journal of Human Rights*, 9, 207–23.

Snappin' Turtle Productions. 2016. Parliament Square Turned Into Lifejacket Graveyard To Raise Awareness of Refugees [Online]. *snappinturtle.co.uk*. Available: www.snappinturtle.co.uk/production-projects/lifejacketlondon/ [accessed 1 July 2018].

Taylor, D. 2003. *The Archive and the Repertoire: Performing Cultural Memory in the Americas*. Durham: Duke University Press.

Thompson, A. K. 2011. The Resonance of Romanticism: Activist Art & Bourgeois Horizon. *In:* Firat, B. M. O. Z. and Kuryel, A. (eds.) *Cultural Activism: Practices, Dilemmas, and Possibilities*. Amsterdam: Rodopi.

Tilly, C. 1985. War Making and State Making as Organized Crime. *In:* Evans, P. B., Rueschemeyer, D. and Skocpol, T. (eds.) *Bringing the State Back In*. Cambridge: Cambridge University Press.

Tilly, C. and Tarrow, S. G. 2015. *Contentious Politics*. New York: Oxford University Press.

Walters, W. 2006. No Border: Games With(out) Frontiers. *Social Justice*, 33, 21–39.

Weber, L. 2010. Knowing-And-Yet-Not-Knowing About European Border Deaths. *Australian Journal of Human Rights*, 15, 35–58.

Weber, L. and Pickering, S. 2011. *Globalization and borders: Death at the Global Frontier*. Basingstoke: Palgrave Macmillan.

Weber, M. 1919/2015. Politics as a Vocation. *In:* Waters, T. and Waters, D. (eds.) *Weber's Rationalism and Modern Society: New Translations on Politics, Bureaucracy, and Social Stratification*. Basingstoke: Palgrave Macmillan.

Wilkinson, S. and Kitzinger, C. 2009. Representing the Other. *In:* Prentki, T. and Preston, S. (eds.) *The Applied Theatre Reader*. Oxon: Routledge.

Wyatt, D. 2015. The Syrian Artist Who Superimposes Western Masterpieces Onto Bombed Buildings. *The Independent*, 8th September 2015.

Žižek, S. 2008. *Violence: Six Sideways Reflections*. New York: Picador.

5 Power v. violence

How can contemporary art create a 'space of appearance' and generate social change?

Jessica Holtaway

Figure 5.1 Hong Kong Intervention
Source: © Sun Yuan and Peng Yu 2009

This chapter looks back at the 2009 artwork *Hong Kong Intervention* by Sun Yuan and Peng Yu to consider the social impact of the artwork and how it changed according to its cultural display. In *Hong Kong Intervention* the artists gave 100 migrant domestic workers a plastic toy grenade and asked each participant to photograph the grenade somewhere within his or her employers' home. The resulting images were exhibited alongside images of the participants with their back to the camera so that they could remain anonymous. The interventions drew attention to political issues around the working conditions and rights of the migrant domestic workers (MDWs) who make up nearly 5% of the population of Hong Kong.

Drawing on Hannah Arendt's idea of the 'space of appearance' (1958: 198, 199) as a potentially transformative political space and Ernesto

Laclau's concept of an 'internal antagonistic frontier' (2005: 74) that can lead to social change, I reflect on *Hong Kong Intervention* and how its tongue-in-cheek yet provocative representation of potential violence was designed to generate sympathy towards migrant domestic workers. Although Arendt and Laclau write from very different social and political contexts, they each explore the idea of power with relation to political engagement.

For political theorist Hannah Arendt, 'power' is distinguished from 'violence'. Power is manifest through individuals acting in concert. She argues that the possibility of acting together to achieve social change is brought about through a 'space of appearance': a space where people gather together to speak and act (Arendt, 1958: 199). Power is 'what keeps the public realm, the potential space of appearance between acting and speaking men, in existence' (1958: 200). The space of appearance is an informal space that disappears when discussion and deliberation ends. Central to Arendt's understanding of politics as praxis is her notion of 'the social' – unthinking mass society. In order to critically evaluate the idea of art providing a 'space of appearance' and particularly in relation to the social positioning of MDWs in Hong Kong, I address the idea of 'the social' with reference to Hanna Pitkin's 1998 book *The Attack of the Blob: Hannah Arendt's Concept of the Social*. Using Pitkin, I explain how some of the complexities inherent in the idea of 'society' are addressed in *Hong Kong Intervention*.

'Power' is a key concept in *Hong Kong Intervention*, and I expand on the reading presented through Arendt's work by considering Ernesto Laclau's idea that an 'internal antagonistic frontier' is necessary to construct affective political discourse. I will suggest that this internal antagonistic frontier sustains the kind of engagement that is required to keep the space of appearance in existence.

In short, through reflecting on the writings of Arendt, Pitkin and Laclau, I want to investigate two main questions: First, from the standpoint of MDWs in Hong Kong, does *Hong Kong Intervention* have a transformative impact? If so, how? Second, how does the cultural display of the artwork affect its potential social impact? Both Arendt and Laclau consider how we might create interstices within prevailing social systems to assert a sense of inter-subjectivity and accountability in relation to specific political concerns. In this chapter I explore how art and art activism might create such interstices – spaces that *intervene* between things, generating power and social change. Looking at the cultural framing of *Hong Kong Intervention*, I go on to argue that the contextualisation of art within exhibition spaces has a significant effect on the potential power of these works.

Hong Kong Intervention

In the gallery space, *Hong Kong Intervention* featured photographic documentation of 100 MDWs and their placement of a plastic toy grenade in the
homes of their employers. Each placement was different – in one image the
grenade was next to the family dog (Figure 5.1). In another it was placed
in the edge of a breakfast bar in an immaculately clean kitchen, or unobtru-
sively on a bookshelf (Figure 5.2). In the Osage Gallery, where the work
was first exhibited, the images of these different placements and the workers who participated in the intervention covered the walls of the gallery,
forming a bold collective presence.

The title of the artwork situates each domestic worker as a kind of
'intruder'. MDWs are required by law to live with their employer. However, although the domestic settings are their home, they are 'outsiders' to
the space. Hong Kong law stipulates that each 'helper'[1] be 'provided with
suitable living accommodation with reasonable privacy' (2007; 'Quick
Guide for the Employment of Domestic Helpers from Abroad'). This varies
according to the discretion of each employer, but it is not unusual for workers to sleep in public areas of the house if they have a screen that provides
'privacy'. It is not uncommon for domestic workers' living space to amount
to a padded cupboard in the kitchen. Aside from these issues of privacy
and space, many MDWs are victims of domestic abuse. And even those
who have space and security in their place of work cannot easily become
Hong Kong permanent residents. Unlike most other migrants to the city,
who can apply to become a Hong Kong permanent resident after living
there for seven years, migrant domestic workers are rarely classed as being

Figure 5.2 Hong Kong Intervention

Source: © Sun Yuan and Peng Yu 2009

'ordinarily resident' in the city and cannot, on the whole, become permanent residents (Ewing, 2018).

A domestic worker occupies a position of trust; as part of a household workers are responsible for preparing meals and, often, caring for children. To draw attention to the possibility of an underlying resentment or a dormant aggression highlights the potential vulnerability of employers and their children, who depend on MDWs for their private domestic needs. In exposing these domestic spaces within a gallery, the artwork not only highlights the subversive potential of MDWs but also uncovers the illusion of privacy within this domestic arrangement.

Sun Yuan and Peng Yu's portrayal of the domestic workers as intruders could be perceived as reinforcing prejudices against domestic workers and antagonising the social issues highlighted so far. How can such a provocative gesture have a political impact that supports MDWs? Patrick D. Flores, Professor of Art Studies at the University of the Philippines, wrote a short text on *Hong Kong Intervention*, which was published in the catalogue for the exhibition. He references Claire Bishop in 'The Social Turn: Collaboration and Its Discontents': 'I would argue that shock, discomfort, or frustration – along with absurdity, eccentricity, doubt, or sheer pleasure – are crucial to a work's aesthetic and political impact' (Bishop, 2006: 181). *Hong Kong Intervention* is bold and discomforting, but the artwork is playful rather than threatening. Each image captures a unique private space and records the aesthetic, often darkly humorous, choices individual domestic workers have taken in situating the plastic grenade. The sense of looking at the scene through the eyes of the migrant worker situates the viewer as complicit in the intervention.

What were the aims of the artists? Sun Yuan speaks critically of 'harmonious society' in which knowledge is 'in sync with the government' (interview with Xu Tan, date not recorded). He says that 'commercialization and the participation of economics contribute to the realization of a harmonious society'. Peng Yu adds that in a 'harmonious society' 'people have to play by the rules and to strive for breakthrough in between. After some time, everybody ends up playing tricks' (interview with Xu Tan). Although the piece could be seen as a 'collective action' – 100 different MDWs participated, albeit separately and in secret – this action is not 'harmonious' because each intervention refers to a political demand. In this piece, the interventions became manifest as a collective action when the images were displayed together and when audiences could potentially speak and act together to address the social dynamics that were being critiqued. By drawing attention to the realities of individuals unified by political aims, the artwork creates an alternative space from which to think about issues of residency and belonging.

In the introductory catalogue text for *Hong Kong Intervention*, curator David Elliott explains that the artwork leads to

> reflections on the nature of power . . . how it is disposed, politically, economically and socially, both in China and throughout the world – and on what role, if any, art may play in channelling, challenging or deflating it. Here the act of representation becomes both a tool and a weapon.
>
> (2011)

How can representation become a tool for social change? This chapter suggests that *Hong Kong Intervention* embodies Arendt's notion of 'power' and demonstrates how an artwork can open up a discursive space that encourages audiences to respond to social injustices.

Cultural display

The social significance of *Hong Kong Intervention* has shifted over time. After the initial exhibition at the Osage Gallery in Hong Kong in 2009, *Hong Kong Intervention* was exhibited in the 2010 Sydney Biennale, at LASALLE College of Art in Singapore and Tang Contemporary Art in Beijing in 2012, and in Art Basel Hong Kong in 2013. How did the changing context of the artwork – from local to global and from a gallery supported by an educational art foundation to an international art fair – alter its impact?

In Singapore, the public response generated financial aid for charities and shelters that support migrant domestic workers. Sustaining and developing independent charities and organisations created greater awareness and perpetuated a sense of accountability. When the piece featured in Art Basel Hong Kong 2013, the significance of *Hong Kong Intervention* shifted again. Exhibited in an international art fair, it became part of a commercial aesthetic discourse.

Sun Yuan comments:

> After this work entered the collection of the Singapore Art Museum, a large part of the proceeds were donated to Hong Kong aid agencies for foreign workers – in particular, the Mission for Migrant Workers, an organisation committed to assisting migrant workers who are in distress, and the Bethune House, a temporary shelter for displaced and distressed domestic helpers of all nationalities.
>
> (Quoted in Bailey, *Hyperallergic*, 2013)

These charities provide practical support for MDWs; they enable individuals to cope with physical and psychological challenges and to gain strength that can enable some individuals to develop the confidence to face the precarity that comes with advancing a political discourse. Additionally, the charities increase the visibility of MDW campaigns, advancing specific concerns within Hong Kong politics. As such, charitable giving is a positive response. Nevertheless, one could argue that responding to the debate by donating money to a charity might not actively generate an incentive for social change. Sun Yuan acknowledged this saying, 'Capitalist methods of donating through charitable means will not erase the guilt' (Hyperallergenic, 2013). Charitable giving provides only partial satisfaction of the demand that the artwork makes – a demand on the part of the workers to mobilise against top down 'violence' through generating collective power – can ultimately become disempowering. Although such a response is well intentioned, it fails to tackle the underlying social order that allows for the exploitation of the workers.

In the context of an art fair, the role of the domestic workers in the piece changed and appears to re-enact the very dynamic it was critiquing in the first place. The domestic workers essentially became free labourers, used to produce a piece of potentially profitable art that no longer had such a critical relationship to the socio-economic system it lies within. In this wider international setting, its audience was more detached from the specific political environment from which it emerged, and although still relevant, its power was diffused. The work 'showcased' Hong Kong art and risked positioning the art as illustrative of, rather than entangled in, a political context. At this point, we might question the ability of the artwork to generate discourses that lead to social change. Although this is possible, it is perhaps less likely to happen.

Here we can see that the power of an artwork can be limited by its cultural display. Although temporal, *Hong Kong Intervention* created cracks or openings within a social 'norm'. These spaces depended not on individuals 'having' power in a conventional sense but on a group of workers voicing demands through the creation of an artwork – an action that generates a powerful space for critical reflection. In this instance, such openings generated further changes, for example in shifting attitudes of audience members towards the domestic worker they employ, increasing solidarity between MDWs by stimulating further ideological ways of communicating political ideas or by providing support for institutions that assist MDWs in crisis. Together, these active approaches become part of a process of empowerment. However, this was a temporary impact, because, when the artwork was exhibited in the art fair, it began to assume a specific value and to become more detached from its original context.

The space of appearance

In *The Human Condition*, Hannah Arendt emphasises the importance of discursive space. She calls it a 'space of appearance' and likens it to the Greek *polis*, in which 'everything was decided through words and persuasion and not through force and violence' (1958: 26). Arendt notes that the *polis* depended in part on the existence of slavery, a strict division between public and private space and unequal gender roles. However, by deconstructing the ides of the polis, tracing the ways in which this space altered over time and focusing on the 'space of appearance', we can begin to imagine a revised, contemporary *polis*.

The traditional *polis* arose from clear differentiation between public and private space. But the nature of this discursive space began to change. As speech and action were gradually 'banished' from public space into the private realm (Arendt, 1958: 49), the power of public speech and action diminished, and the idea of 'the social' emerged. For Arendt, 'the social' has become an all-encompassing realm in which predictable 'behaviour' has replaced 'action'. She writes that 'the social' demands the kind of consensus of 'an enormous family which has only one opinion and interest' (Arendt, 1958: 39). At the same time the emergence of 'the social' has changed traditional approaches to 'the household' leading to a greater focus on *individual* speech and action and weakening platforms for collective action. Acknowledging the demise of the traditional *polis*, Arendt forwards the idea of the 'space of appearance' as a non-violent discursive space that allows individuals to come together and speak and act in a way that generates social change though collective action.

Having described 'the social' as an all-encompassing phenomenon, a 'final stage' in social development in which 'society has devoured all strata of the nation and "social behaviour" has become the standard for all regions of life' (Arendt, 1958: 45), there seems, on the surface, to be little hope for existence outside of 'society' as such. Arendt says that 'what makes mass society so difficult to bear is not the number of people involved, or at least not primarily, but the fact that the world between them has lost its power to gather them together, to relate and separate them' (1958: 52–3). Is it possible, then, to regain such power and to create spaces of appearance? To answer this question, we need to address the possibility of deconstructing Arendt's concept of 'the social'. Hanna Pitkin explores and critiques the idea of 'the social' in her 1998 book *The Attack of the Blob: Hannah Arendt's Concept of the Social*.

Pathways into 'the social'

Pitkin begins the book by critiquing the way that Arendt creates a perception of society as a distinct entity, by turning the adjective 'social' into a noun – 'the social' – rather than using the word 'society'.[2] Pitkin states: 'Arendt herself warned against the sort of mystification in which she nevertheless engaged – ascribing the results of human action to some abstract personified agency beyond human influence' (1998: 6). In emphasising the sheer force of social inclinations and trends, it is easy to interpret Arendt's concept of the social as a kind of superhuman entity. Pitkin creates a kind of caricature of what she understands Arendt's 'social' to be – an extraterrestrial 'blob' taking over the world. This image could be misleading because, although Arendt often uses language that hints towards a personified 'social' entity,[3] she clearly understands it as a collectively formed phenomenon and one that 'found its political form in the nation state' (1958: 26). Pitkin argues: 'By 'the social' Arendt means a collectivity of people who – for whatever reason – conduct themselves in such a way that they cannot control or even intentionally influence the large scale consequences of their activities' (1998: 16). However, if we look at the concept of the social in the wider context of Arendt's writing, we can see that she does not visualise 'the social' as a separate entity but rather as a large-scale shift in relationships allowing dictatorial roles to flourish. We might then alter just one word of Pitkin's analysis and exchange 'cannot' for 'do not' so that the sentence would read 'a collectivity of people who – for whatever reason – conduct themselves in such a way that they *do not* control or even intentionally influence the large scale consequences of their activities'. Drawing attention to potential agency within the concept of the social helps us avoid perceiving it as a specific and hybrid form that is 'beyond human influence'.

Arendt and Pitkin both essentially defend the agency of people to choose to address and control, to a greater or lesser degree, the consequences of their activities. Pitkin acknowledges this difference when she herself adds 'do not' and writes in her conclusion that 'the social' should be understood as the 'absence of politics where politics belongs, a condition in which a collectivity of people – who for whatever reason – cannot (or at any rate do not) effectively take charge of overall resultants of what they are severally doing' (1998: 252). These words clarify the underlying message of Arendt's concept of 'the social' and begin to move away from any characterisation that we might be tempted to project on to it. Pitkin goes on to say that the overall point

> is not so much whether Arendt saw the details of our institutional situation aright, or whether I do, but that we need to reconsider our institutional forms and structural conditions with a view to reducing the social and enlarging the possibilities for freedom.
>
> (1998: 260)

Pitkin articulates different 'paths' *into* the 'problem of the social' – approaches that create a distance between oneself and 'society'. These 'pathways into the thicket of the social' (Pitkin, 1998: 253) do not exist outside or circumvent 'the social'; they create spaces within it that perhaps allow for the emergence 'of politics where politics belongs' (Pitkin, 1998: 252).

First we have the institutional approach. For Arendt, 'the social' can be characterised by two models of organisational structures – free-market economy and bureaucracies. Alternatively, she defined a 'council system', an institutional model that can be understood as a power structure that is generated by 'the people' (Pitkin, 1998: 12, citing Arendt's *On Revolution*, p. 223). Pitkin extends this idea and stipulates that to achieve it 'such local bodies must be small and accessible to all who want to participate', and they must also 'have something meaningful to do and must have or be able to acquire sufficient power to make a real difference in matters that affect participants' lives' (1998: 257–8).

The second approach is a 'characterological approach'. Pitkin reminds us that 'the institution [of the social] *is* the conduct – the habitual, structured conduct of people 'in' it' (Pitkin, 1998: 261). She says that 'if a sufficient number of those in it share that deviancy, the institution will . . . already *be* changed' (1998: 261). Such a deviancy, however, requires courage – a value highly regarded in the *polis* – and realisation of one's agency that leads to having a sense of responsibility. For Arendt, this arises from a love of the world, of the people that make up the world. But Pitkin concludes that for such a personal approach to the world to be effective it must somehow intersect with the institutional pathway that we have just discussed and become part of a public discourse.

Ideologies are explored in the third approach. One of Arendt's greatest concerns, following her coverage of the Eichmann trial, was that of 'thoughtlessness', a word that Pitkin understands as a 'misguided mode of thinking' rather than a complete absence of thought (1998: 270). In contrast, direct interaction with others, through which we endeavour to understand their perspectives, leads to an empathic engagement with the complexities of their experiences. Arendt develops this sense into a political form and advocates the importance of critical thinking. Without it, she believed that the world falls under ideological illusions. Pitkin describes these as 'deliberately imposed policies of unreality to which those who impose them eventually themselves fall victim' and that this idea is central to totalitarianism (1998: 272).

The fourth approach Pitkin outlines, 'just do it', requires 'thinking as an actor' and involves becoming part of a collective commitment, 'not one more rival explanation or policy prescription but more like an essential supplement to any and all of the other approaches (to the social), more about how they are to be employed than an alternative to them' (1998: 281). Pitkin emphasises the need for each path into the social to be enacted and lived by people. She reminds us that, for Arendt, action is the activity that constitutes the world (1998: 283), but this cannot depend simply on isolated actions; it requires individuals to act as part of a group. Pitkin states that 'the problem of the social, however, is that people are power without having it' (1998: 292). If we understand that this can also be true of those creating pathways into the social, it can also be the beginning of a solution to the 'problem of the social'.

Pitkin summarises this alternative approach to institutional and structural models by outlining the need to create 'institutions that facilitate creative initiatives from below' and that encourage 'widespread deliberation about public affairs that connects public policy to what really matters to people' (1998: 260). The idea of deliberation, as a characteristic within such institutions, is key to generating and sustaining the possibility of 'spaces of appearance' – spaces that allow speech and action to characterise reality.

How do these 'pathways' illuminate how *Hong Kong Intervention* embodies spaces, utilising them as 'spaces of appearance'? 'The institutional path' accesses the social though large organisational structures and though interpersonal relationships and conduct. For *Hong Kong Intervention* this initially took place through the institution of the gallery, where both the participants (the MDWs that took part in the project) and the audience within the gallery are required to respond to the work. In this way, an art exhibition is open to all who wish to participate – to engage with ideas presented through the artwork – although not everyone can be a part of the formation of the work. One of the institutional outcomes outlined by Sun Yuan was the support generated for established charities. Although Sun Yuan describes this as an ideal outcome, he reminds us that charitable giving cannot 'erase the guilt' (Hyperallergenic, 2013). As discussed earlier: charitable giving does not necessarily change underlying power structures that lead to the need for charitable giving.

'The characterological approach' utilises personal relationships and the psychology of individuals. In terms of *Hong Kong Intervention*, the formation of the project, before it became formalised as an artwork, required courage on the part of individual MDWs enacting the interventions. Although essentially playful, the interventions and the disclosure (albeit veiled) of the workers themselves (and the interior spaces) lead to the risk of being recognised. The participants are essentially risking their job and therefore their right to remain in Hong Kong. But because there were so many interventions, the power and significance of the piece increases, and the collective force of the work has a greater presence within the public space. However, to achieve this collectivity required the structured oversight by the artists, and their negotiation with the Osage Gallery.

'The ideological path' uses concepts and frameworks of ideas to approach the social. *Hong Kong Intervention* calls attention to a social hierarchy and an assumed relation of trust inherent within this. In doing so it calls it into question the ideologies that support or fail to acknowledge the nuances and consequences of such a social structure. The artwork plays with the idea of a potentially violent intrusion – it acts antagonistically. In other words, it abruptly demands critical thinking as a response to the images. Pitkin talks about the need for a 'reciprocal' relationship; she believes that the capacity to relate and interact with others in a balanced way is crucial for politics (1998: 266). But to obtain the attention of others in the first place, a point from which to then develop ways of interacting and relating, often requires such a provocative gesture.

The 'just do it!' approach requires thinking as an actor rather than just thinking about action. It is a call to acknowledge one's agency (Pitkin, 1998: 253–84). Peng Yu reflects this idea in an interview in *Randian* where he speaks of the thought processes behind their artistic practice as a whole, saying that their work 'intervenes directly in reality' but that it 'doesn't have a clear direction' (interview with Liang Shuhan, 2013). *Hong Kong Intervention* does not advocate for specific policies; rather, it asks the audience to think as actors. The artists 'consider all the participants as collaborators: not just Filipinos, but also the audience involved in the discussions' (interview with Wendy Ma, Art Radar Journal, 2009). The audience members are participants in the artwork. And the artwork, rather than asserting a specific ideology, demands that audiences question accepted attitudes towards MDW and the political policies that affect them and think as responsible actors.

The collective response of both the MDWs and the audience define *Hong Kong Intervention* and create a powerful potential for social change. Initiating an active approach to the pathways into the social enables these pathways to be progressive spaces. This is manifest, not by individuals having power but by consciously being part of a powerful social shift. Such an active approach might be characterised by a change in approach of audience members towards the domestic worker they employ, an increase of solidarity between MDWs, providing support for institutions that assist MDWs in crisis or campaigning with MDWs. Together, these active approaches have more power.

Power, antagonism and the space of appearance

Returning to Arendt's statement that 'power is what keeps the public realm, the potential space of appearance between acting and speaking men, in existence' (1958: 200), the chapter now considers the question of how to sustain a potential space of appearance. It outlines how power relates to the space of appearance, with reference to Laclau's writings on the construction of the political. This section considers the relationship between the 'people' and power and explores the possibility that demands can be unified, even as difference continues to operate.[4] It looks at Laclau's concept of a 'broken space' that allows antagonisms to maintain the radical openness of a space of appearance. It draws parallels between this space and Pitkin's 'pathways' into the social and relates this to *Hong Kong Intervention*.

How does the concept of 'power' relate to 'the space of appearance'? In *The Human Condition* Arendt understands power as what keeps the space of appearance in existence, and she states that power is always 'a power potential and not an unchangeable, measurable and reliable entity like force or strength. . . . Power springs up between men when they act together and vanishes the moment they disperse' (1958: 200). Therefore, it is closely connected to the concept of the space of appearance and depends on the ability of a group to act in concert and to generate power through collective action. In other words, the space of appearance is characterised by a 'mode' of collective engagement.

In *The Crisis of the Republic* Arendt emphasises the difference between 'power' and 'violence'; 'The extreme form of power is All against One, the extreme form of violence is One against All' (1972: 141). She explains the idea of power as an 'end in itself' and compares this to the concept of 'peace', saying that just as we cannot answer the question 'What comes after peace?', we cannot understand power in finite terms. In contrast, she explains that violence is often justified by its ends (1972: 150). It lacks the legitimacy that power requires but can still be justifiable. She says that violence is 'more the weapon of reform than of revolution' (1972: 176). *Hong Kong Intervention* might be understood as a 'powerful' gesture rather than a 'violent' one – it functions collectively and depends on the communication of a past action in order to perpetuate further speech and action. The project itself had no violent potential, but by enacting and representing the social tensions at play for the participants, it created a 'power potential' that opened up a discursive space within the social environment of the artwork.

Sun Yuan stated in the catalogue for the exhibition, '[a]lthough the artwork is merely a final product for the project, what we believe, however is that the idea behind would transcend itself to be a model that can be implemented by others, of what we call an "intervention"' (Sun Yuan and Peng Yu, catalogue text, 2010). In its approach to the political dilemmas at stake, the project aims to encourage a shift in underlying attitudes towards MDWs rather than rectifying specific concerns or proposing a particular reformative approach. Their aim was to create a model of interaction, rather than a clear-cut solution. For the project to have power, it needed to sustain plurality and accommodate opposing responses to the exhibition, whilst providing the possibility for a unified response that acknowledges the MDWs as individuals with rights.

Ernesto Laclau's writings on political engagement also address the idea of power with relation to collective action. For Laclau, 'the people' (understood as 'a real relation between social agents' (2005: 73)) mobilise *against* the possession of power, through the articulation of a 'demand' (2005: 73). Here there is a shift in the conceptualisation of power – Arendt thinks of power as something that bubbles up through a collective demand, but Laclau refers to an existing power structure that can be weakened through the articulation of a demand (by the people). However, this difference does not undermine the significance of 'spaces of appearance', which we can also understand as sites where 'real relations between social agents' begin to form. And it is this *process* of sustaining relations between social agents that is important when considering the political significance of an artwork such as *Hong Kong Intervention*.

Laclau writes of the necessity of an 'internal antagonistic frontier' (2005: 74) that perpetuates a continual need to establish and re-establish links between people. This 'frontier' prevents the crystallisation of 'the people' into a group that is simply 'against' something. For Arendt, power is essentially 'a power potential'. It arises from the mode of collectivity, one that is discursive and shifting, rather than adhering to an ideology. This antagonistic frontier means that 'power' in Arendtian terms is not something that is considered a natural by-product of a collective but is understood as something that can be created by the political mode of communication between individuals that allows for the emergence of 'the people' through the 'equivalential articulation of demands'.

Laclau speaks of 'equivalential bonds' and the importance of a 'discursive identity that serves as the equivalential link'. Rather than representing democratic demands themselves as equivalent (2005: 93), Laclau says that 'difference continues to operate within equivalence, both as its ground and in a relation of tension with it' (2005: 73). In this context, we might understand that 'the social', having absorbed both the public and the private realms, does not allow for the articulation of demands and often assumes and dictates these demands.

But how can the people retain this kind of dynamic political power, which requires difference in order to operate, whist simultaneously unifying their demands? Laclau states that the goal of populist movements is to create a 'stable system of signification' (2005: 74). A system that generates, perpetuates and encourages the negotiation of demands can allow for open political discourse to operate through stable and constant avenues. Such a system can act as a 'reliable' mechanism that produces power. Within the space of appearance, the signifying mechanisms of speech and action constitute the space, but there must be conditions that make this possible. The space of appearance relies upon certain systems of signification – signs that can call people together or identify a lack. However, its core purpose is not to foreground one rationale above another but to create an open space for political engagement. As such, it can often be perceived as vague and conflicting. Laclau aligns himself with Rancière and refers to 'the essential asymmetry at the root of popular action' (2005: 93). For Laclau, the contingency of difference operating within unification is key to creating a more nuanced and discursive political awareness.

The space of appearance depends on vocalising and performing asymmetries and differences. A contemporary space of appearance is defined by 'antagonistic frontiers', and the need for 'asymmetry' at its root. Likewise, art can become a site for an 'antagonistic frontier' if it creates a platform for oppositional forces and asks questions, rather than reducing a situation or scenario to an essence or simple meaning. At the same time, for it to be accessible and for questions to be articulated and communicated, there will inevitably be a frontier between this space and 'the social'. Familiar visual signs can be used to communicate with individuals who are swallowed up in the social.

Laclau outlines the 'dimensions of a broken space' (2005: 85) and defines three conditions. First, there must initially be a 'lack'; a 'gap' in 'the harmonious continuity of the social'. In *Hong Kong Intervention* the lack of rights for MDWs is the political foundation for the piece. Second, the need for order becomes more important than the ontic order that produces it; Laclau describes the 'asymmetry between ontological function and its ontic fulfilment' (2005: 87). This is addressed in the artists' intention to create a 'platform for conspiracy' (Hyperallergic, 2013) that has greater significance than the separate aesthetics of each intervention. And third, there is a tension between difference and equivalence, which is at the heart of *Hong Kong Intervention* – the piece antagonises the social tensions between the need for MDWs and the potential threat that collective action on the part of the MDWs might mean economically. Laclau says that 'democratic demands are, in their mutual relations, like Schopenhauer's porcupines'; they need to remain close to each other to keep warm during the cold weather but they harm each other if they come to close each other. Although desiring a mutual relationship, they are unable to achieve it without injuring the other (2005: 85–9). These dimensions, although considered just briefly here, help us to appreciate the idiosyncratic and precarious nature of such a space.

To summarise, Arendt states that the space of appearance requires people to act and speak together, and Laclau pushes this idea further and says that the way that people act and speak together is the key to creating a discursive identity. He says that there must be an 'internal antagonistic frontier' that separates 'the people' as power (in Arendt's terms) from 'power' and allows difference to operate within equivalences. For this frontier to be antagonistic and able to affect the fundamental nature of the system it opposes, there must be an 'antagonistic moment', which evades 'conceptual realisation' by circumventing a perceived sequential logic that the opposing system assumes or depends upon. This evasion allows the antagonistic moment to be 'constitutive' and able to form a radical frontier.

Laclau echoes Pitkin's imagery of 'pathways into the thicket of the social' through his description of the 'antagonistic moment' as a 'chasm'. For Pitkin, politics emerges in the spaces within the social that are created by thoughtful engagement. She says that such engagement, whether it is through institutional, characterological or ideational means, 'can have further, widening effects, enlarging the space for freedom' (1998: 283). Both Laclau and Pitkin explore the creation of fractures and 'clearing' or 'breaking' spaces within the wider social environment. We can therefore begin to understand that unlike the *polis*, which was a space 'outside' defined in contrast to private space, the contemporary space of appearance is a space 'within' that manifests itself as a kind of fissure within the social. Although this space occurs within the social, it appears as if created by an external force, a logic or approach independent from 'the social'. This external force makes inroads into the social, which offsets the borders between interior and exterior space and weakens the constancy of 'the social'. Here I am suggesting that we adapt Arendt's illustration of 'the social' to recognise the porous nature of the social realm and our agency within it. Focusing instead on Arendt's idea of the 'space of appearance' in a contemporary context and alongside insights from Pitkin and Laclau, we can start to recognise how micro-political transformations can unfold within social systems that seem to exert an overwhelming 'power', in Laclau's terms, or 'force', in Arendt's.

The contemporary space of appearance borders political, social and cultural territories, but is not a constitutive a part of pre-formed territories. It does not aim at a specific outcome, although it can provoke institutional changes. The purpose of the space of appearance is to create a discursive space through the generation of 'power potential' and for this space to facilitate a 'stable system of signification' that allows for a discursive mode of political engagement to weaken 'the social' and increase the possibility of political change through 'bottom-up' politics.

Conclusion

The aim of this chapter was to explore ways in which contemporary art can have political agency by creating spaces of appearance within dominant

social paradigms. First it looked at how *Hong Kong Intervention* had a transformative impact, and second it considered how this impact was affected by
its cultural display. It presented *Hong Kong Intervention* as an artwork that
was able to generate contemporary spaces of appearance – spaces that spark
social change through collective speech and action. But it also recognised
how its cultural display affected the potentiality of this space.

It explored the idea that a contemporary space of appearance acts as a
kind of 'fissure' within a social norm. Drawing from the writings of Hanna
Pitkin, it highlighted four pathways into 'the social'. It considered the need
for an empathetic approach to others and emphasised the importance of
creating links between people so that power can be generated through collective engagement. It considered the role of institutions as points of contact
within society that can increase the possibility of advancing into 'the social'
and described the way in which *Hong Kong Intervention* created paths into
the social environment in which it was exhibited, through 'institutional',
'characterological', 'ideological' and 'active' approaches.

As such it suggested that the space of appearance occurs as a break in
'the social'. It is this emergence of a space in its 'breaking' or 'appearing'
that implies an externality. For this space to have agency and for it to resist
absorption into 'the social', it must continue to have what Laclau calls an
'internal antagonistic frontier'. It must continue to have internal antagonisms and points of resistance that perpetuate open dialogues. Therefore,
a space of appearance is not a place of escape or for relaxation – such a
space does not provide reconciliation but instead amplifies a sense of plu-
ral existence and the possibility for social change. It looked at *Hong Kong
Intervention* as a model of intervention and antagonism – it embodied an
approach to a political situation that allowed for difference to operate within
equivalences.

Key to the concept of the 'space of appearance' is Arendt's understanding of 'power' as radically different from 'violence'. Such power is not a
means to an end. Whilst violence is often justified by a particular outcome,
this concept of power cannot be articulated in finite terms, and this is what
perpetuates the possibility for change and the freedom to imagine alternative realities. Power is something we can potentially share.

The contemporary space of appearance occurs and operates differently
from the way in which the *polis* functioned. This chapter suggested systems
of representation that might act as mechanisms to produce potentially political spaces and open new platforms for political engagement within contemporary society. It outlined how interventions into different socio-political
contexts can create spaces of appearance. However, we might now ask:
How can such cultural tools function collectively? How might these spaces
overlap, perpetuate or even conflict with each other? How might we map

out the multitude of pathways within the social and investigate the political impact of possible intersections and collaborations?

Notes

1 The Hong Kong government term for migrant domestic workers in English is 'domestic helper'.
2 Pitkin states that this is something that Arendt does not do with the word 'political'.
3 Some active verbs she uses to describe what society 'does' are 'demands', 'banishes', 'devours' and 'destroys'.
4 For Laclau, the word 'demand' in the English language is particularly appropriate because it is ambiguous – it can mean both a request and a claim. He says that within a 'demand' 'the transition from a request to a claim provides a defining feature of populism' (2005: 73).

Bibliography

Arendt, Hannah. *Crises of the Republic: Lying in Politics; Civil Disobedience; On Violence; Thoughts on Politics and Revolution* (Boston: Houghton Mifflin Harcourt, 1972).

Arendt, Hannah. *The Human Condition* (Chicago: University of Chicago Press, 1958).

Bailey, Stephanie. 'The Artists Who Gave Domestic Workers Toy Grenades', *Hyperallergic*, May 23rd, 2013, http://hyperallergic.com/71441/the-artists-who-gave-domestic-workers-toy-grenades/ [last accessed May–August 2013].

Berkowitz, Roger, Jeffery Katz and Thomas Keenan (eds.). *Thinking in Dark Times: Hannah Arendt on Ethics and Politics* (New York: Fordham University Press, 2010 edition).

Bickford, Susan. 'The Paradox of Public Appearance', in *Feminist Interpretations of Hannah Arendt* (Pennsylvania: Pennsylvania State University Press, 1995).

Biglieri, Paula and Gloria Perelló. 'The Names of the Real in Laclau's Theory: Antagonism, Dislocation, and Heterogeneity', http://filozofskivestnikonline.com/index.php/journal/article/viewFile/104/110 [last accessed June 2013].

Bishop, Claire. 'The Social Turn: Collaboration and its Discontents', February 2006, *Artforum*, pp. 179–85.

Chan, Yuan-Kwan. 'Sun Yuan and Peng Yu: Hong Kong Intervention – Art Basel Hong Kong', *Meniscus*, May 23rd, 2013, www.meniscuszine.com/articles/2013052323295/sun-yuan-peng-you-hong-kong-intervention-art-basel-hong-kong-2013/ [last accessed August 2013].

Elliott, David. 'Somewhere Beyond Rape and Adultery: the Development and Work of Sun Yuan and Peng Yu', August 2011, Hong Kong, www.sunyuanpengyu.com/other/HK%20Intervention_Catalogue_19August2011.pdf [last accessed May–August 2013].

Ewing, Kent. 'High Court Ruling on 'Live-in' Rule Guarantees Further Abuse of Hong Kong's Domestic Workers', *Hong Kong Free Press*, 2018, www.hongkongfp.com/2018/03/04/high-court-ruling-live-rule-guarantees-abuse-hong-kongs-domestic-workers/ [last accessed October 2018].

Flores, Patrick D. 'Embedded', August 2011, Hong Kong, www.sunyuanpengyu. com/other/HK%20Intervention_Catalogue_19August2011.pdf [last accessed May–August 2013].

The Government of the Hong Kong Special Administrative Region of the People's Republic of China. 'Quick Guide for the Employment of Domestic Helpers from Abroad', www.immd.gov.hk/ehtml/ID(E)989.htm [last accessed August 2013].

Laclau, Ernesto. *On Populist Reason* (London: Verso, 2005).

LASALLE college website, 'Hong Kong Intervention', www.lasalle.edu.sg/Events/ EventDetail.aspx/Hong-Kong-Intervention [last accessed August 2013].

Law, Lisa. 'Defying Disappearance: Cosmopolitan Public Spaces in Hong Kong', http://usj.sagepub.com/content/39/9/1625.short [last accessed August 2013].

Ma, Wendy. 'Surprising New Direction Taken by Cadaver Artists and Saatchi Stars: Sun Yuan and Peng Yu – Interview', *Art Radar Journal*, September 16th, 2009, http://artradarjournal.com/2009/09/16/surprising-new-direction-taken-by-chinese-cadaver-artists-and-saatchi-stars-sun-yuan-and-peng-yu-interview/ [last accessed August 2013].

Pitkin, Hanna Fenichel. *The Attack of the Blob: Hannah Arendt's Concept of the Social* (Chicago: University of Chicago Press, 1998).

Shuhan, Liang. 'Interview with Sun Yuan', trans. Daniel Szehin Ho, *Randian*, March 15th, 2013, www.randian-online.com/np_feature/interview-with-sun-yuan/ [last accessed August 2013].

Tu, Xan. 'Xu Tan Interview to Sun Yuan & Peng Yu', www.sunyuanpengyu.com/ article/other/xutan.html [last accessed August 2013].

Index

Printed in the United States
by Baker & Taylor Publisher Services